S

BROOKLYN

*Michelle Young and Augustin Pasquet
in collaboration with T.M. Rives*

PHOTOS
Augustin Pasquet with T.M. Rives

JONGLEZ PUBLISHING

travel guides

In the last couple of decades, Brooklyn has been "rediscovered", but those that have lived here for generations have always known that the borough is full of history, hidden spots and cultural dynamism. New Yorkers have been relocating to Brooklyn in droves, in search of a place that still feels like the city they grew up in. New transplants and residents alike come seeking affordability and community. Tourists have found the borough's edgy coolness irresistible.

The Brooklyn of old stood as its own city, and that tradition of independence means that today, there's something for everyone. There are skyscrapers as tall as those in Manhattan, quaint brownstone-lined streets and even suburb-like neighborhoods. This guide is for those that want to go beyond the tourist path, past the Brooklyn waterfront neighborhoods, though there are many secrets to be found there too. The locations featured in this book will take you from the very northern tip of the borough to the heady amusement parks of Coney Island; to an architecturally award-winning wastewater treatment plant on the northern edge of Brooklyn; to a rock that marked the border of Queens and Brooklyn; to the wonders of central Brooklyn; and to the beginnings of an underwater train tunnel to Staten Island that was never completed.

Brooklyn's history reveals itself in the present day and the sheer size of the borough means there's plenty to discover. Some of our favorite highlights include a grocery store frozen in time from 1939, a rooftop vineyard, and a fair share of both abandoned and reactivated locales. There are the quirks of history, still standing amidst modern development, like the oldest building on Coney Island and the remnants of the motion picture industry, which had its start in Brooklyn. Then there are the modern day finds, like a secret writing room of a Superhero Supply Store or a state of the art cheese aging initiative inside historic beer tunnels. And there are the mysteries, still unsolved, like an 1836 locomotive, possibly trapped behind a wall under Atlantic Avenue. There are also numerous unusual activities to partake in, like a safari to see the wild monk parrots that live on the streets of Brooklyn or a food foraging tour of Prospect Park.

Enjoy!

We have taken great pleasure in drawing up *Secret Brooklyn* and hope that through its guidance you will, like us, continue to discover unusual, hidden or little-known aspects of the borough.

Descriptions of certain places are accompanied by thematic sections highlighting historical details or anecdotes as an aid to understanding the borough in all its complexity.

Secret Brooklyn also draws attention to the multitude of details found in places that we may pass every day without noticing. These are an invitation to look more closely at the urban landscape and, more generally, a means of seeing our own city with the curiosity and attention that we often display while travelling elsewhere …

Comments on this guide and its contents, as well as information on sites not mentioned, are welcome and will help us to enrich future editions.
Don't hesitate to contact us:
  Jonglez Publishing, 25 rue du Maréchal Foch,
  78000 Versailles, France
  E-mail: info@jonglezpublishing.com

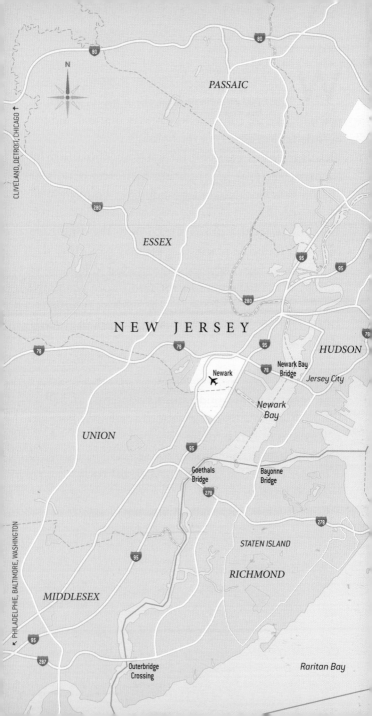

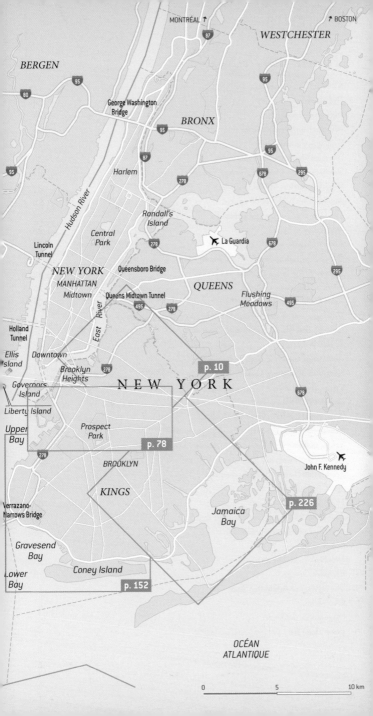

MONTRÉAL ↑   ↗ BOSTON

WESTCHESTER

BERGEN

George Washington
Bridge

BRONX

Harlem

Randall's
Island

✈ La Guardia

*Central
Park*

Lincoln
Tunnel

NEW YORK
MANHATTAN
Midtown

Queensboro Bridge

QUEENS

Queens Midtown Tunnel

*Flushing
Meadows*

Holland
Tunnel

Ellis
Island

Downtown

p. 10

East River

*Brooklyn
Heights*

N E W   Y O R K

Governors
Island

Liberty Island

*Upper
Bay*

*Prospect
Park*

p. 78

John F. Kennedy ✈

BROOKLYN

KINGS

p. 226

Verrazano-
Narrows Bridge

*Jamaica
Bay*

*Gravesend
Bay*

Coney Island

*Lower
Bay*

p. 152

*OCÉAN
ATLANTIQUE*

Hudson River

0   5   10 km

CONTENTS

To the north

Brownstone belt and beyond

CONTENTS

Down south

East to the borough border

To the north

York. The names of their big bosses will be familiar: Lucky Luciano, Bugsy Siegel, Meyer Lansky. These guys made their reputation and money moving alcohol during Prohibition and in racketeering after the repeal of the 18th Amendment.

The hitmen of Murder Inc. are estimated to have carried out anywhere between 400 and 1000 contract killings, using all available methods and tools. A preferred weapon was the ice pick, which was not only an efficient and easily available murder device, it was also particularly feared. A New York City police detective told *The New York Times*, "Murder is not only to take somebody's life away, but to terrorize ... 'Do you want to wind up in a landfill somewhere, stabbed with an ice pick?' That was the message that went out to the people who didn't comply with the rules of the Mafia."

During its heyday as ground zero for Murder Inc., this corner spot was the Midnight Rose Candy Store, a 24-hour coffee and sweets shop run by a woman in her 60s. Rosie Gold had a row of telephones, which were used by the syndicate to organize the hits. The gangsters would wait in the candy store until the phone rang with instructions. The location was considered ideal – next to the elevated subway train line, with windows onto the street for lookout purposes.

Rosie was clearly in on the take and evidence shows she was involved in a loansharking business with Abraham Reles, the man who would take Murder Inc. down. In the book *Bummy Davis vs. Murder, Inc.: The Rise and Fall of the Jewish Mafia and an Ill-Fated Prizefighter*, author Ron Ross writes, "It was not uncommon for the containers in Rose's freezer to be filled with vanilla ice cream, chocolate ice cream, and a couple of pistols cooling down."

In 1940, Reles was caught by a police informant and turned on his Murder Inc. colleagues, most of whom would face the electric chair at Sing Sing Prison. Reles came to an equally terrible end, falling down seven floors from the Half Moon Hotel in Coney Island while under police supervision – likely a revenge killing for ratting. Through all of this, the only person in Murder Inc., who appears to have made it scot-free was Rosie Gold.

THE KNICKERBOCKER FIELD CLUB

A 19th-century tennis club hidden behind a series of apartment buildings

114 East 18th Street
Brooklyn, NY 11226
www.knickerbockerfieldclub.net
Early May to December (check website for hours)
Transport: B/Q subway to Church Avenue

South of Prospect Park, off Ocean Avenue, is a short, two-block street with a "punny" name: Tennis Court. Most people who pass by probably chuckle and move on, if that. But Tennis Court was originally part of a larger development, much like nearby Prospect Park South and Flatbush-Ditmas Park, with Victorian-style detached homes set amidst lawns and gardens. But the true secret gem of Tennis Court lies just across 18th Street: an actual historic tennis club hidden behind a series of seven-story apartment buildings. Still, nothing celebratory denotes the existence of the club along the street, beyond a small green sign atop a roll-down gate entrance. But walk through the parking lot and you'll discover five original

clay courts in pristine condition that date to the founding of the club in 1889. The Knickerbocker Field Club was part of a land lease from Ronald Ficken, a developer who pioneered real estate development in the Flatbush area in the mid-1880s. The secret tennis club is the only remnant of the Tennis Court development, which originally spanned several square blocks.

The club was wildly successful from its inception, attracting prominent Brooklyn families as members, including many women. Today there are 170 members with over 100 people on the waiting list. According to the club officers, it takes up to ten years to get a membership, at $900 per season.

On a visit, when asked why people come from a distance to play here, one of the members called out "Because it's the best!" Another member, Beth Moorsmith, says, "It's partly the history, because this place has been around for so long. And it's partly that it's *so* New York." Her husband Reid adds, "There are no fancy pretensions. People like to play tennis. Despite the fact that it's surrounded by brick buildings and a subway, it feels like an oasis."

The club originally had a Colonial Revival-style wood clubhouse, built in 1892. The building, designed by Partfitt Brothers, a respected Brooklyn-based architectural firm, was landmarked by New York City in 1978, when it was the only building from the Tennis Court development still standing. The clubhouse was severely damaged in 1988 in an arson fire, and despite its landmark status, was approved for demolition due to financial hardship. A smaller clubhouse was built in its place.

Today, the Har-Tru clay courts see active use, with the club open five days a week. "The best thing about the club besides the tennis courts [is] the people," says Raymond C. Habib, the president of the club, "It's the members that keep people here." On a visit, the sense of community and camaraderie is clear. Just don't expect to be part of the club anytime soon.

Free junior programs
Famous tennis players and pros come to give clinics on occasion, and there is a free junior program every summer for six weeks.

NEARBY
Albermarle Terrace ⑥
On the other side of Ocean Avenue from the Knickerbocker Field Club and Tennis Court is a tiny historic district that encompasses just two residential courts. The charming tree-lined streets, particularly Albemarle Terrace, feature handsome, beautifully-maintained neo-Federal style row houses. With the development of Flatbush Avenue into a bustling commercial corridor, the discovery of this historic district, one of the smallest in New York City, is a delightful, architecturally pleasing surprise.

THE PIETER CLAESON WYCKOFF HOUSE

The oldest building in New York City

5816 Clarendon Road
Brooklyn, NY 11203
718-629-5400
www.wyckoffmuseum.org
Grounds open Friday–Saturday 12pm–4pm and most weekdays
House tours by appointment only

Built by Peter Wyckoff, who settled in Dutch New Amsterdam in 1637, the Pieter Claeson Wyckoff House has many superlatives to its name. Most notably, dating from 1652, it is the oldest building in New York City. Wyckoff came from a place called Norden, now located in modern-day Germany and spoke Frisian rather than Dutch. When he arrived in the New World, he worked as an indentured servant on the Rensselaerswyck estate, a vast property one million acres in size. After six years, he became a tenant farmer and married a Dutch woman.

In 1652, the couple purchased land south of Rensselaerswyck in Nieuw Amersfoort in present-day Canarsie. They built a simple structure with one room and earthen floors. Wyckoff became a successful farmer and local magistrate, and the house was expanded and altered over the years.

Only a small portion of the house dates to 1652, most was added in the 19th century. Today, there are six rooms, three fireplaces, an attic and a cellar. With a pitched, sloped roof, it is thought to be the oldest example of a Dutch saltbox frame house in the United States – a style common in the Colonial era.

On December 24, 1976, the Wyckoff House was the first building in New York City to be designated a historic landmark. The house is a museum run by the New York City Parks Department, and is a member of the Historic House Trust, which claims that the Dutch farmhouse "exemplifies the diversity of Brooklyn's colonial farms, where Dutch-American landowners, enslaved and freed Africans, and later European immigrants labored on some of the country's most

fertile land." Eight generations of the Wyckoff family lived in this house until 1901.

All the Wyckoffs in America and Canada (who spell their name in numerous forms: Wycoff, Wykoff, Wikoff, and Wicoff) are believed to be descended from Pieter Claeson Wyckoff and his wife, who had eleven children. With the English takeover of New Amsterdam, Pieter was obliged to add a last name. He chose the name of a place in Germany (Wykhof) where he had lived with his parents. Wyckoff descendants collectively bought the house in 1961 to turn it into a museum.

GOLDEN GATE FANCY FRUITS AND VEGETABLES GROCERY STORE

There is simply no other place left in New York City like this

2080 Flatbush Avenue
Brooklyn, NY 11234
Transport: B41 Bus to Flatbush Avenue/Avenue P

"**Y**ou've just stepped into 1939," says John Cortese, the 92-year-old proprietor of Golden Gate Fancy Fruits and Vegetables. Indeed, the old-school grocery is far more authentic than any Hollywood set designer can create and it's located way off the beaten path. It's a true neighborhood establishment, in operation at this same spot in Marine Park since 1939, when it was opened by John's grandfather. John would do the deliveries after school and recalls getting followed

by stray dogs who would surround the produce upon hearing the squeaking of his cart.

John is a World War II veteran who served in the invasion of Normandy and the Battle of the Bulge as part of the 551st Field Artillery Battalion. No detail escapes his memory; from the names of towns he passed through in France and Belgium to the model number of the metal detector he used in the war.

He talks of the pre-war era as the "good old days," and recounts the prices back then. Newspapers were two cents, a hot dog (onions, ketchup, and all) was five cents, as was a subway or trolley ride. Though prices have changed, the inside of the grocery remains virtually the same as it did when it opened.

The wood floor, with its narrow boards, is original, as is the tin ceiling. Cans of Goya beans and Redpack crushed tomatoes sit on painted shelves. Produce is displayed beautifully on angled stands and atop wooden crates that line both sides of the store. Two scales still hang from the ceiling, just in case of a power outage. Original Sunkist advertisements, old-school product labels that John saved, and a plethora of vintage photographs decorate the store.

In the back room are some true gems: a pot belly heater, a wooden cold storage room, and a Triplex gas stove, all still working. Even the exterior sign, with its faded hand-painted lettering, dates to the mid-century. Take note of the old telephone number, ES-7-2581, a format used from the '40s to the '60s.

Though you might assume everything is kept for the nostalgia, John assures it's not. He wanted to redo the storefront decades ago, but his accountant told him that as a result, they'd need to get new floors, new stands, new everything. So they just kept it the same.

And as for the name? John isn't even sure himself. The Golden Gate Bridge opened in 1938, a year before the shop did, and John surmises the shop might be named in its honor.

These days, John keeps the shop going to stay busy. "I've been around a long time," he says, before handing us a bag of delicious peaches and cracking a joke. He opens at seven in the morning and has breakfast in the back room with a locksmith friend from nearby. He plays music from earlier decades on his vintage radio, and though his dancing days might be over, he just might sing a tune for you. His son pitches in at the store sometimes, as does his grandson – three generation of Brooklynites named John Cortese.

There's a lot of love here, between family, friends and the community, and even the care taken by John over the produce quality and the merchandising. The result: there is simply no other place left in New York City quite like Golden Gate Fancy Fruits and Vegetables.

UNDERGROUND RAILROAD SPOTS ⑨
AT THE HENDRICK I. LOTT HOUSE

Little known slave history in the "closet within a closet"

1940 East 36th Street
Brooklyn, NY 11234
718-375-2681
Open for special events and tours
Transport: Q35/B46 Bus to Flatbush Av/Utica Av, B2 Bus to Fillmore Av/East 36th Street

Built originally in 1720 in the middle of quiet Marine Park, the Hendrick I. Lott House was expanded (and possibly moved some feet over) in 1800. Two hundred acres of the land in this neighborhood, originally the town of Flatlands, used to belong to the Lott family. The house was the longest continuously owned home by a single family in New York City.

The last resident, Ella Suydam died in 1989. The house became abandoned and within a decade, it was deteriorating from the elements. It was also a popular spot for local teenagers, who dared each other to go into the "haunted" house.

Today, it's one of those old houses, full of secrets rooms and curious spaces. The current caretaker discovered a trap door by accident, hitting her head on the ceiling of a closet. There used to be a staircase through the trap door that led to two garret rooms. Under the floorboards, items were found that belonged to the slaves that once lived and worked on this land. There's also a basement level with a crumbling old stove and pens for dairy animals.

But the true secret of the house, staunchly kept within the family into the late 20th century, was the "closet within a closet"; the Lott's freed their slaves about two decades before the state of New York abolished slavery and it is believed that the house was later used as a stop on the Underground Railroad, helping escaped slaves reach freedom in northern United States and Canada.

Through a door behind one of the parlor rooms, turn up a winding staircase to the second floor rooms. Inside the first room on the right, there's a closet under the gabled roof. Within it, a second doorway leads to a small crawlspace. Originally, the closet would have been filled with possessions, concealing this second doorway and the secret space. Dates on old New York newspapers that cover the inner wall of the closet are still visible. Several say 1862, printed just a few weeks before the Battle of Gettysburg.

Alyssa Loorya, an urban archaeologist and founder of Chrysalis Archaeological Consultants, serves as Vice President of the board of the Lott House Preservation Association. She says that a location for the Underground Railroad stop here makes sense. Gerritsen Creek used to come up closer to the Lott House, which is en route to Weeksville, a neighborhood in Brooklyn founded by freed slaves in present-day Crown Heights. Heritage New York "made the determination that there is enough circumstantial evidence to say that yes, it could have been a stop on the Underground Railroad," Loorya says.

The city purchased the home from the Lott family in 2001, saving the house from possible demolition and the land from being subdivided. It's a New York City landmark and is currently undergoing rehabilitation to both the house and the surrounding property.

REMAINS OF THE GERRITSEN GRIST MILL

The first tide-powered mill in North America

Just east of the Marine Park Salt Marsh Nature Center, viewable only at low tide
Transport: B44 Bus to Avenue U/Nostrand Avenue

Gerritsen Creek gets its name from the Gerritsen family, early Dutch settlers who inhabited this area of Brooklyn for three

5-7 FRONT STREET BUILDING

The oldest office building in New York City

5-7 Front Street
Brooklyn, NY 11201
Transport: A/C to High Street, F to York Street

Unnoticed by the throngs of tourists waiting for a slice of pizza from Grimaldi's or Juliana's, 5-7 Front Street is believed to be the oldest office building in New York City.

The three-story building was constructed in 1834 in the Greek Revival style, built as the offices for the Long Island Insurance Company.

As old newspaper reports show, it was a rather lively building with many tenants. The ground floor was first occupied by Hart's Bank Coffee House, which hosted meetings for the Kings County Democratic Republican General Committee and was an official election polling place. The ground floor was home to a grocery in the 1850s, owned by a Brooklyn councilman. A barber shop was located here for at least half a century beginning in 1864. Its proprietor, a German immigrant called Mr. John Anton, served clients as famous and varied as Reverend Henry Ward Beecher, Brooklyn Bridge builder John Roebling, and Boss Tweed.

As noted by the Landmarks Preservation Commission in the 1977 designation of the Fulton Ferry Historic District, what makes this building particularly notable architecturally is that it was "still quite unusual in the early part of the 19th century" when it was built though it is of a style that is now quite common to New York.

RED HOOK LANE

②

The only section left of a Native American trail

372 Fulton Street
Brooklyn, NY 11201
Transport: A/C/F to Jay Street-Metrotech, 2/3/4/5 to Borough Hall

Today, Red Hook Lane is a one-block road located nowhere near the neighborhood of Red Hook. It runs diagonally from Fulton Street to Livingston Street and almost got de-mapped completely in 2004 to allow for the construction of a large building. But the anomalous road still remains today, a disorienting find until you know its history.

As could be expected, Red Hook Lane once stretched to Red Hook. Created before the arrival of the Dutch and the British, the road began as a Native American trail used by the Canarsie Indians. Considered one of Brooklyn's oldest roads, it also served as a key means of access during the American Revolution for troops on both sides of the war. American militiamen found it an ideal spot to shoot at British troops using the road.

Local historian John Burkard was the driving force behind the creation of the Red Hook Heritage Trail: secondary signs that were added to ten intersections in Red Hook in 2008. The signs reignited awareness of Red Hook's role in the Revolutionary War, a place Burkard claims is the "birthplace of America" because it enabled the retreat of George Washington's troops. Many of the old roads and military installations are long gone, including Fort Defiance, which is marked only by a plaque along the waterfront and as the name of a popular local bar and restaurant.

Back in downtown Brooklyn, a flatiron building at 127 Livingston Street had stood at the southern tip of Red Hook Lane since the 19th century. The red building was a recognizable landmark for many years, with a subway-inspired mural painted by Steve Powers. The street art piece located subway stations like "Meh," "So Long" and "Nope," as well as "Hero Shop" for the sandwich store at the bottom floor. It was sadly demolished in 2015.

Only time will tell what the next iteration of Red Hook Lane will look like, but if history is any indication, the street will be here long after the buildings have gone.

MASSTRANSISCOPE

Illusion on the Q train

Q train and B train, Manhattan-bound after the DeKalb stop; only visible on the right side of the tunnel

S o weak is the impulse to look out the windows of a subway car in motion, most commuters, many Q-train and B-train regulars included, have no idea that the tunnel leading from DeKalb station to the Manhattan Bridge contains one of the city's most clever and hypnotic works of public art: *Masstransiscope*. *Masstransiscope* is a series of lighted panels that make the gloomy concrete walls suddenly gush and twitter with colorful abstract shapes that fold and morph, apparently suspended in the dark.

One part of the charm of *Masstransiscope* is that it's one of the only pieces of subway art that does something. The other part is: that something is illusory. The work is based on the zoetrope, the first contraption to take advantage of the human eye's persistence of vision to create apparent motion, frame by frame – the principle behind all film and animation. *Masstransiscope* takes this concept and cunningly reverses it. The brightly colored animation isn't really doing anything at all: *we* are, by moving. The successive frames are always out there, passive, inert, whether passengers are flying by or not. One interesting effect of this can be seen if the train lags after leaving the station: the animation stalls as the frames break into the narrow slits of colored light they've always been. Then the train picks up speed, the slits warp into action, and *Masstransiscope* smoothly hovers and morphs again.

"I think it was such a preposterous idea that no one bothered to say no," said Bill Brand, creator of the work. Brand, an artist and filmmaker, began pitching the project in the late 70s and finally installed the panels – 228 in total – in 1980. If his original idea had been realized, the animation would be changed from time to time to create constantly fresh experiences. But it's been hard enough to maintain as it is; Brand used to have to descend into the tunnel by an abandoned station to make his own repairs. Still now, after a full 2008 restoration and a 2013 rehabilitation, you might see only a portion of the work on any one trip, but even a few flickering seconds are worth the trouble.

METROPOLITAN CHAMPIONSHIP

Gateway to boxing glory

130 Water Street, Brooklyn, NY 11201
718-797-2872
www.gleasonsgym.net
The Metropolitan Tournament is held in late fall

Gleason's Gym, Brooklyn's temple of pugilism, offers dozens of events during the year. It's the home of White Collar Boxing, where amateurs are given a venue to beat the hell out of each other in front of a crowd; it has weathered the shift of the neighborhood to higher-rent with strenuously hybrid programs like *Strike!* ("boxing/chamber music/dance concert"). But if you want the purest dose of the blood–sweat–tears potion that transforms the sport into a metaphor for personal struggle, come watch the Metropolitan Tournament.

The guys call it "The Metro." It's the last major hurdle before the country's most elite contest, the Golden Gloves, and the fighters, many as young as 15, rightly see it as a gateway with a vision of glory shimmering on the other side. The youths radiate a unique vibe: swaggering, methodical, nervous. Each is looking to improve his "book," the record of wins and losses that will decide a career. Once in a while a brawler will come off the street with enough raw talent to make a mark quick. "That's what you look for," says Elmo, a trainer. "They're the ones that bring the excitement." More often it comes down to sweat. A Rockaway boxer, swinging his fists as he awaits his turn at the physical check, agrees. "You could be talented," he says, "but a person who works hard will beat you any day. *Any day.*" These are some of the most disciplined teenagers you will ever meet.

Show up before the bouts start and you can follow the personal stories: the background narrative that will culminate in a crash of guts and strength in the ring. "I'm two–three," says Jonathan, shadow boxing with fresh white tape on his hands. That's two wins, three defeats. A look of controlled worry passes over his face. "Wait, no: two–four." Another fighter sits on the edge of the ring, already gloved up, spitting on the floor with studied nonchalance. George, just 15 and a first-timer at the tournament, sulks back from the weigh-in to his trainer. "I'm a pound and a half over," he says. The trainer hands him a jump rope. "You got fifteen minutes. Lose it." Asked if a person can really shed a pound and a half in fifteen minutes, the trainer shrugs: "Yeah," with the unspoken note that it depends on how much you want to. In the end George doesn't. Glory packs up her laurels and leaves quietly out the back door.

SEINING IN THE EAST RIVER

Life in the shadow of the bridge

718-222-9939
https://www.brooklynbridgepark.org/
May to September
Held at the foot of the Manhattan Bridge (Brooklyn Side)
Transport: F train/York St; A and C trains/High St

Seining, the research fishing technique used by Brooklyn Bridge Park Conservancy, involves wading out into the waves and dragging shoreward a 20-foot net (a "seine") with very fine mesh. Whatever was minding its natural business out there gets swept up and laid out for review in the shallows on the beach (and later thrown back). The East River, just something to be crossed over or under in a train for most New Yorkers, is an estuary rich with life that outdates us by millions of years. Blue and striped bass, pipe fish, marine snails, crabs, shrimp, eels … "We mark down everything," says Nick, an environmental science student who handles one side of the net, "so we can understand exactly what's in there, per season and per year. It's a great way to monitor the health of the river and instruct the public."

The place to do this is the small inlet where the Manhattan Bridge meets Brooklyn. The place is like a theater, and the show is New York's essential forces: out across the river rises the dramatic skyline, inland is a grassy park bracketed by the relics of the area's historic industry: brick warehouses and factories. A wooden jetty, bristling with rusty nails, makes a rickety reach for the water; on the other side is the eastern stanchion of the titanic bridge: faded blue iron, chains hanging from the underbelly. Pick your way down the granite seawall at low tide and you'll discover a minute sandy beach where, on weekends, you can explore this part of the scene that would otherwise remain mysterious: life down under the river's surface.

The public is heavy on kids, who watch the net come in with excitement spiced with just a hint of nerves: there's no telling what haunts the deep in the shadow of a great bridge. Plastic buckets filled with water are set out for the more interesting creatures; brave kids touch and handle them. "Why isn't it snapping?" asks a boy about a shore crab. "Because it's too small," says marine biologist Nim Lee, talking through a portable mic system so she can be heard above the serial thunder of trains passing overhead. The crab's spindly legs tread air between her fingers as she holds it up for display. "He would love to snap me, but I'm bigger." The boy frowns down at his own hand as if to compare. Later, he whispers confidentially: "A crab can snap your finger *off*." It's what they call starting the conversation.

BROOKLYN HEIGHTS FRUIT STREETS

Lady Middagh's vendetta

Cranberry, Orange and Pineapple Streets
Brooklyn
Transport: A/C to High Street

In November of 1965, the Brooklyn Heights Historic District became the first landmarked district in New York City under the city's new landmarks preservation law. Walking through the handsome neighborhood today, it may be hard to imagine that there was once significant concern that the area was deteriorating historically. Some blocks were even "taking on the character of slums," as stated in the landmark designation report.

This state of affairs would have been shocking to the original residents, who built mansions and beautiful houses on these quaint streets. Many of the streets were named for the wealthy families who settled here: Montague, Joralemon, Pierrepoint, Remsen, Schermerhorn, to name a few. Yet when you walk through the streets near the Columbia Heights waterfront,

you'll encounter three streets named after fruits: Cranberry, Orange and Pineapple. Legend has it that a Lady Middagh of the Middagh family, a pre-Revolutionary-era family that owned the land roughly between Fulton Street, Hicks Street and Tillary Street, waged a nomenclature war against her other upper-class neighbors. The official New York City Parks sign at the Fruit Street Sitting Area gives Lady Middagh a slightly less vindictive nature, stating that she found the street naming convention "pretentious". This kinder reasoning does not, however, explain why Middagh Street remained.

Regardless, Lady Middagh is said to have taken down the street signs and replaced them with those named after fruits. When the city replaced her signs, she would put up new ones. This continued for a while until the city accepted the fruit streets, making them official by decree of an alderman. It is unclear exactly when this took place, but the First Village Map of 1816 already has the fruit streets labeled. Lady Middagh did allow Henry Street to remain (named after the Middagh family doctor) and kept the street named for her family.

On these fruit streets today, which lead out to the Columbia Heights promenade, you'll find a nice historical mix of wooden clapboard houses and stately townhouses, along with some of the large apartment complexes that were built before the district was landmarked.

From The New York Public Library

REMNANTS
OF THE HOTEL ST. GEORGE

The vestiges of once NYC's largest hotel

100 Henry Street
Transport: 2/3 to Clark Street ; A/C to Hight Street

I t isn't easy to tell today, between the scaffolding and significant architectural changes that have taken place, but the Hotel St. George in Brooklyn Heights was once one of the largest and grandest hotels in New York City. Built between 1885 and 1929, it was a hotspot for celebrities such as Truman Capote, Duke Ellington, Leonard Bernstein, and Presidents Roosevelt and Truman. It had a rooftop Egyptian nightclub, 17 ballrooms, and a pool renowned for its ornamentation and use of salt water.

The Hotel St. George still sits in the heart of Brooklyn Heights, its former lobby converted into the entrance to the Clark Street subway stop. Transit-goers steam in and out of it daily, most unaware of its full history.

A large portion was converted into co-ops in the 1970s and 1980s. The once celebrated hotel had fallen into disrepair, housing what the New York Times described in 1995 as "a number of homeless people and AIDS patients — placed there by city agencies." That year, most of the interior of the Hotel St. George complex was destroyed in a massive fire accidentally set by a con-man who was scavenging for copper in the building. The blaze required 500 firefighters to put out. The Hotel St. George has been further subdivided into dormitory housing.

But if you look closely, there are still some neat remnants to discover at the building. One of the most obvious is the original entrance awning found on Clark Street and Henry Street. Most of the original lobby, which contained a grand staircase and marble pillars, was parceled off to a developer in 1984. It was converted somewhat haphazardly into the only entrance of the Clark Street subway station. Most of this entrance corridor is nondescript, even run down, with exposed fluorescent overhead lights, mismatched wall tiling, and functional businesses.

One item that appears to have remained in the subway entrance from the hotel days is the Cutler metal mailbox. It carries the original logo of Cutler and a Gothic-style eagle, which remained in use until the 1930s.

On the corner of the building at the intersection of Clark Street and Henry Street is a neon sign: "LIQUOR STORE HOTEL ST. GEORGE." The wine shop below it, Michael-Towne Wines & Spirits, first opened in 1934 as Town Wine & Spirits, the 65th store to obtain a license to operate in New York State following the repeal of Prohibition.

Finally, though the pool has been converted into a gym, the original green tiled columns and mosaics are still present, a find first reported by the website Scouting NY. After finding these, an even juicier remnant was discovered: the original pool still exists below the current one. Someone who worked on the renovation stated, "The pool still exists. We were not allowed to nail, chip, or remove any part of the original pool complex. We ran sleepers (beams) across the pool and floor area and built the new floor on the sleepers. The new pool is suspended from this floor, set into the larger existing pool."

PLYMOUTH ROCK
AT PLYMOUTH CHURCH

A piece of the first piece of America

Plymouth Church of the Pilgrims
75 Hicks Street, Brooklyn
718-624-4743
www.plymouthchurch.org
Church office open weekdays 9am–5pm
Transport: 2 and 3 trains/Clark St; A and C trains/High St

Plymouth Church, built in the mid-1800s, has been called Plymouth Church of the Pilgrims since 1934 when it merged with the nearby Church of the Pilgrims. Both were Congregational, and founded by New Englanders. When the Church of the Pilgrims packed up, before leaving they took hammer and chisel to their bell tower and broke out a stone – a rough chunk of granodiorite about a foot across – and carefully moved it to the new location on Orange Street.

The stone is an original piece of Plymouth Rock. Plymouth Rock, in case you napped through elementary school, is supposedly the very spot in Massachusetts where the first pilgrims landed on the Mayflower in 1620. You can see the fragment today in the church gallery, sitting like a statue in its own niche, which turns out to be the ideal arrangement for lending a chunk of rock an aura of mysterious power. And it has power: it's perhaps the closest anything comes to a physical piece of the myth of America. When the fragment was ceremoniously installed in 1940, Mayor Fiorello LaGuardia said in a speech to the congregation that "the courage and determination of the Pilgrim Fathers" were the qualities most needed in a world at war, as though strength could be absorbed directly from the stone by standing near it.

"There are supposedly three pieces approximately this big," says Lois Rosebrooks, who gives tours of the church. "The one here, one in the Midwest, and one on the West Coast." This is all the more surprising given the size of the original Plymouth Rock in Massachusetts: little bigger than a coffee table. "In the 1700s water was eroding the Plymouth shoreline," Rosebrooks explains, "and they were afraid that the rock was going to be lost. So they hitched up their oxen and pushed and pulled – and it *broke*." The date was in fact 1774; the people of Plymouth took the break as a portent of independence, left the "British" half in the sea, and installed the other in front of the meeting house under the banner "Liberty or Death". Eventually the halves were reunited and displayed in an enclosure at sea level. In the meantime many fragments were lost, some chipped off as "souvenirs," others – like the one at Plymouth – freely given.

Another Plymouth Rock fragment

There's another, apple-sized Plymouth Rock fragment on display under glass in the reading room of the Brooklyn Historical Society, three blocks away at 128 Pierrepont Street.

THE DOORS OF OUR LADY OF LEBANON

⑨

Saved from a sunken ship

113 Remsen Street, Brooklyn
718-624-7228
www.ololc.org
Transport: 2 and 3 trains/Clark St or Borough Hall; N and R trains/
Court St; 4 and 5 trains/Borough Hall

The medallions on the bronze doors of Our Lady of Lebanon Cathedral have a strange theme in common: the architecture of Normandy, France. Does it make sense for the entrance of a Maronite church founded by Syrians in a Romanesque Revival building constructed for New England immigrants to make a thing of French castles? As it turns out, not really. The story:

The Church of the Pilgrims on Remsen Street was designed by one of the city's legends, Richard Upjohn, architect of Trinity Church. When the congregation merged with nearby Plymouth Church in 1934, a large piece of Plymouth Rock was removed from the bell tower (see page 52) and the doors and stained glass windows were torn out with it. Ten years later the mostly Aleppine congregation of the Roman Catholic Church of Our Lady of Lebanon bought the stone building, and the church's resourceful monsignor, Mansour Stephen, took on the job of decorator. The marble and onyx he got from the World's Fair pavilions of France and Lebanon, the windows from stained-glass innovator Jean Crotti. The great bronze doors were bought at auction, courtesy of a recent disaster: the sinking of the SS *Normandie*. The monsignor might strike you as a bit of a savvy operator. "He was amazing," says Father James A. Root, the current rector of the cathedral. "He used to drive, I believe, a Rolls Royce. He was friends with every judge and lawyer and businessman in town."

The transatlantic ocean liner *Normandie*, nicknamed the "Queen of the Seven Seas," was the most powerful steam turbo-electric passenger ship in history. In 1933, *Popular Mechanics* magazine called it "the largest moving unit ever built by man," and went on to note "rare and common woods from all parts of the world; soft and cunningly woven fabrics; works of art that give an atmosphere and refinement to the surroundings." Most interesting to the history of Brooklyn Heights were the bronze doors leading to the dining room: they were decorated with medallions, each depicting a Norman city: Dieppe, Alençon, Falaise. The legendary ship was docked in New York in 1942 when it caught fire, burned, and sank. Much of the interior was sold at auction – just in time for a monsignor in need of imposing cathedral doors. But he bought more than that. "My dining room table is the captain's table," says Father Root, who lives next to the cathedral. "We eat at it every day."

58 JORALEMON STREET

A townhouse hiding a subway entrance

*Transport: N and R trains/Court St; 4 and 5 trains/Borough Hall;
2 and 3 trains/Clark St*

Lower Joralemon Street in Brooklyn Heights has got everything for the contented urbanite: cobblestone paving, shady plane trees and maples, and on either side handsome townhouses with flower planters. Dog-walkers take the sidewalk nice and easy; joggers headed for Brooklyn Bridge Park wave mid-stride to toddlers in strollers. It's the kind of place horror-movie writers like to curse with a sinister secret. It's got something like that, too.

On the south side of the street are three Greek revival townhouses that are structurally identical; you might walk by a hundred times without noticing anything amiss. Numbers 56 and 60 have neat brick faces and white window casings, and an attitude of tranquil habitation. The house between them is an impostor. The front steps are chipped, the basement level is shielded by armor plate, the evenly painted exterior seems to be trying to blend in but the "brick" color comes off as a powdery oxblood. The real tell is the windows: properly speaking, there are none. Number 58 casts a blind, black gaze on Joralemon Street.

"It freaks some people out when they walk by it," says a resident of Number 56. "I've never seen or smelled any weird stuff, but if you hang out here long enough you'll see people come and go in there." These people coming and going aren't furtive vampires, they're employees of the Metropolitan Transit Authority. The townhouse is no house at all: it's a camouflaged subway evacuation tunnel.

The ruse has been going on for decades. Most people on the street have figured out the real identity of Number 58; a very sharp passer-by might guess. The black front doors are cold to the touch: thick steel. The lock isn't your average item: it's made to accommodate some sort of hefty triangular key. There's a crack of air between the doors through which you can see a cheerless corridor lit by a bare bulb. The address also houses large ventilation fans, and after they were installed residents reportedly heard ominous moaning. A neighbor directly across the street says he doesn't mind living around MTA infrastructure; the secret tunnel has been quiet for years. But once in a while someone will get too curious and the police will arrive "in a second." Fair warning.

ATLANTIC AVENUE TUNNEL

The oldest subway tunnel in the world

The backroom inside Le Boudoir
135 Atlantic Avenue, Brooklyn, NY 11201
347-227-8337
www.boudoirbk.com/

For years, intrepid explorers looking to get a glimpse of the world's first underground transit tunnel (built in 1844) could sign up for a tour with Bob Diamond, one of Brooklyn's most quixotic self-made urban archeologists. After dodging traffic and waiting for the lights to change, guests would descend one by one through a manhole removed off the middle of Court Street and down a ladder. They'd emerge into a cavernous space over 2,500 feet long.

Diamond discovered the Atlantic Avenue tunnel in 1980, a remnant of a subterranean portion of the Long Island Railroad that connected New York to Boston. This portion of the line existed before the London Underground system was dug in 1863 and was in place before New York City's first subway, Alfred Ely Beach's pneumatic service, opened in 1869. The Atlantic Avenue tunnel was placed below ground to prevent deadly street level accidents between pedestrians and the trains in the already bustling neighborhood. The tunnel was sealed off in 1861, following a new policy that prevented steam locomotives from running in Brooklyn.

Diamond first became intrigued by the lost tunnel after hearing a radio show about *The Cosgrove Report*, a book that describes actor and future Abraham Lincoln assassin John Wilkes Booth hiding pages of a novel in a tunnel near the Brooklyn Academy of Music. Diamond convinced the Brooklyn Union Gas Company to give him access. He didn't find the notebook but he did discover the tunnel behind a dirt and a concrete wall. He did the excavation himself and has been fighting for the last 30 years to use the tunnel to revive trolley transportation and create a museum. A series of controversies and lawsuits halted Diamond's progress and the tunnel was closed off to tours in 2010.

Diamond believes that there is an 1836 locomotive buried in the tunnel: an engineering firm confirmed through an electromagnetic imaging scan that there was a large metallic object, about the dimensions of the lost train, behind the wall. Diamond himself has lost access to the tunnel and most New Yorkers are skeptical that this portion of the tunnel will ever be opened to the public again.

However, a recent excavation, below the restaurant Chez Moi at 135 Atlantic Avenue, has uncovered a former coal room of the Atlantic Avenue tunnel. Unlike the main tunnel, this space can be accessed as part of Le Boudoir, the speakeasy that opened in 2016 below the restaurant. With stone walls and a barrel-vaulted ceiling, this special room in the back of the hidden cocktail bar has the feel of a grotto. Look up and you'll see the former coal hole, fitted with a new decorative cover by the owners. The walls are still stained by the coal, a detail the owners deliberately left.

In lieu of hopping down a manhole, Le Boudoir is the easiest way to experience the historic Atlantic Avenue tunnel up close.

OLD SUBWAY CARS AT
THE NEW-YORK TRANSIT MUSEUM

Nostalgia underground

Corner of Boerum Place and Schermerhorn Street
718-694-1600
www.web.mta.info/mta/museum
Tuesday–Friday 10am–4pm, Saturday–Sunday 11am–5pm
Transport: 2/3/4/5 to Borough Hall

At the corner of Boerum Place and Schermerhorn Street, a standard subway entrance actually leads down into a decommissioned IND subway station. Closed in 1941, it's been accessible to the public since 1976. It houses the New York Transit Museum, which presents exhibits and programming on the city's transportation system and history. Exhibits have included an in-depth look at resilience and emergency response to natural and manmade events, such as Hurricane Sandy and 9/11; a look inside the secrets of a former transit system headquarters; and an overview of music albums covers shot in the New York City subway system, to name a few.

But the overlooked gem within is located on the lower level of the Transit Museum, where two active tracks host rows of vintage subway cars. Even seasoned New Yorkers have visited and left without heading down the steps, as there is already so much to see on the upper level.

The vintage train collection, which often rotates, contains cars that operated on the subway system when it consisted of three separate companies – the IRT, IND and BMT – and cars from the Long Island Railroad system. The oldest is the BRT Brooklyn Union Elevated Car from 1907, a wooden train that riders would enter and exit via open-air vestibules on the ends of the cars. A BMT car from 1908, the last wooden train to run in America, is shown in the same blue and orange colors it sported for the 1939 World's Fair.

Amidst the old signage of the former Court Street station platform, you can walk in and out of the trains – which are all decorated with vintage advertising – and even sit on the chairs. Seeing the wicker seats, historic fans, and fabric strap hangers is a real nostalgia trip.

You'll also find maintenance trains that serviced the subway system, including the money train that collected the fares, along with various artifacts related to the operation of the subway system. While on the lower level, don't miss the active signal tower behind the first set of stairs. This room controls the movement of trains in and out of this station and tracks the current location of in-service trains at three stations nearby. You can step inside the room but don't touch the board and control switches – it's live!

The Transit Museum's 'Platform' event series features site-specific performances by New York City residents inside the vintage subway cars and on the platforms. All creative fields are welcome. The common denominator is an interest in public transportation.

VESTIGES OF THE GAGE & TOLLNER RESTAURANT

Brooklyn's former most famous restaurant

372 Fulton Street
Brooklyn, NY 11201
Transport: A/C/F to Jay Street-Metrotech

In the middle of a stretch of budget retailers on Fulton Street is a brownstone building with a strikingly handsome portico entrance. Inside, discount clothing and jewelry hide beautiful architectural details that once graced the space. 372 Fulton Street was once home to the famed restaurant Gage & Tollner, frequented by icons such as Truman Capote, Mae West and Jimmy Durante. The building was built in 1875 and the restaurant operated here from 1892 until the mid 1990s. It was a place where New York City's elite families and the celebrities of the day dined amidst elegant surroundings. A 1930 restaurant guide proclaimed that "Gage & Tollner is to Brooklyn what the Statue of Liberty is to New York Harbor," and another guide went so far as to say it was "Brooklyn's main contribution to civilization."

The building is both an interior and exterior landmark of New York City, the first dining establishment to be designated as such. The designation report states, "Gage & Tollner is one of the very few interiors in the City, open to the public, which so successfully project the atmosphere of the 'Gay Nineties.' Upon entering one is immediately transported to the period of Diamond Jim Brady," – the Gilded Age business tycoon.

The Downtown Brooklyn area experienced a general decline in the late 1970s and 80s. The building was lauded in its landmark designation for being carefully preserved but its usage in recent years has concealed its historical significance. It has been both a T.G.I. Friday's and an Arby's, and has had several incarnations as a retail store, but has kept its Gilded Age details behind shop fittings and products. Rows of arched mirrors framed with cherry wood trim line three sides of the long space. These mirrors once created a sense of spaciousness for the restaurant, which is only 25-feet-wide.

The walls are still covered in embossed, bronze-colored Lincrusta-Walton material with ornate patterning. The restaurant was believed to be the only one in the city to have had both gas and electric lighting, and the original brass chandeliers still hang in the store. A wraparound wooden bar, moved from the original Gage & Tollner restaurant at 302 Fulton Street still exists here, overrun by coats and jewelry.

In good news, the redevelopment of the Downtown Brooklyn area in the last couple years has encouraged the owners to re-establish a restaurant in the space. A crowdfunding campaign was started in 2018 by several local restaurateurs to revive Gage & Tollner; thus far it has not reached the $400,000 goal.

FLIERS' AND EXPLORERS' GLOBE

A century of daring

American Geographical Society
32 Court Street, Suite 201, Brooklyn
718-624-2212
www.amergeog.org
Monday–Friday 9am–5pm
Transport: 2, 3, 4 and 5 trains/Borough Hall; N and R trains/Court St;
A, C and F trains/Jay St – MetroTech

In the corner of a small office in Brooklyn sits a fascinating one-of-a-kind object hardly anyone visits. The Fliers' and Explorers' Globe bears the signatures of pilots, divers, mountain climbers, submarine captains: those who went furthest, deepest, fastest, or got there before anyone else. It's the résumé of a century of daring adventure.

Founded in 1851, the Society first headquartered in Washington Square before moving to a fine neoclassical temple uptown at West 156th Street. The Society's first members were some of the wealthiest educated men in the city at a time when throwing money at hair-raising expeditions was a gentlemanly pursuit. Members could sit in a leather chair before the Society fireplace and discuss the strangeness of the Arctic Circle while the men they'd sent there shivered in the white night, boiling their last sled dog. As knowledge advanced and the world grew less mysterious, geography lost its appeal. The Society moved operations to humbler offices on Wall Street, and when those became too costly, to the fluorescent-lit second floor of a high-rise overlooking Borough Hall that it shares with law offices, a hair stylist, and a shoe repairman. The great irony of the American Geographical Society is that over the years it has become increasingly difficult to locate.

"We're just kind of hanging in there, 160 years later," says Peter Lewis, the current director. "This used to be the place where you could come and look at the greatest holdings of charts and maps in the world. Now," in a glass-half-full tone of voice, "you can come and take a look at the globe." The Fliers' and Explorers' Globe goes back to 1929, when Society president and *Times* editor John H. Finley began taking it down to the wharf to intercept returning explorers. They signed the surface, turning the globe into a totem of human courage. Wiley Post, first flight around the world. Amelia Earhart, first woman to fly the Atlantic solo. William Beebe, who dove 3,028 feet in a bathysphere. As the tradition took hold, the globe also inducted earlier explorers like the first men to reach the Poles: Robert Peary (North) and Roald Amundsen (South).

Now there are nearly 80 signatures. The feats associated with some of the names, for example Neil Armstrong, would have made the original founders choke on their cognac.

"LOST COLUMBUS" OF CADMAN PLAZA

Lost and found. And lost. And found. And lost ...

Columbus Park, Cadman Plaza, Brooklyn
Between Court, Johnson, Adams and Joralemon Streets
Transport: 2, 3, 4 and 5 trains/Borough Hall

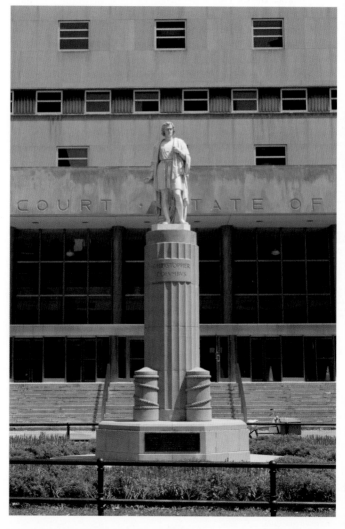

I n all, there are six statues of Christopher Columbus in New York City; the one in Cadman Plaza has the honor of being the first. It also has, by a very wide margin, the most convoluted history.

"MARBLE COLUMBUS IS REDISCOVERED," reads a headline from the *Times* on March 14, 1912. "A $25,000 Statue, Forgotten for Twenty Years, is Found in Central Park." The imagination places the statue under vines and leaves and the trunk of a fallen tree; the truth is less cinematic. The marble Columbus turned up in the corner of a pub. For two decades, the article reads, "it has stood in the main restaurant of McGown's Pass Tavern, scarcely noticed by the crowds who assemble there. A dusty American flag has been stuck between the right arm and the body."

The 1912 "discovery" was actually the second time the statue had been found in a dark corner gathering dust. The work was sculpted in Rome in 1867 by Emma Stebbins (better known for the angel in Bethesda Terrace) and formally presented to the park, which seemed pleased to accept it: comptroller Andrew H. Green praised the "genius of the American sculptress." All the more strange that we later find, in a guide to Columbus monuments, this comment on Stebbins' 4-ton explorer: "The statue has never been erected, and is now stored in an old arsenal in the zoölogical garden." The guide is from 1892, the quadricentennial of the discovery of America and otherwise a big year for Columbus statues (Columbus Circle; the Mall). When it was printed that a perfectly good but superfluous Columbus languished in storage, it was hauled out, put on display for a short time, and then somehow banished to the park's uptown backwater to be ignored by tavern drinkers.

But, as though subject to persistent curse, before the statue found its way to Brooklyn it would be lost yet a *third* time. "FORGOTTEN STATUE FOUND IN PARK YARD," reads the headline from 1934. After McGown's Tavern, the Columbus had been misplaced in another dismal nook, this time a maintenance yard at 97th Street. It was finally removed from the park that had so completely neglected it, given a new base, and, after a stint in Chinatown, landed in Cadman Plaza. The marble statue has a nice open spot in front of the Supreme Court Building, with lots of sunlight, or lots of rain, or lots of snow, or what have you – but for now at least, no more dust.

CRASHGATE AND TUNNEL ENTRANCE TO THE MTA'S SECRET MONEY ROOM

A clandestine subway tunnel for money

On the F line platform of the Jay Street subway station
Transport: A/C/F to Jay Street-Metrotech

370 Jay Street is part of the NYU Downtown Brooklyn campus today, but it once served a very clandestine role within the New York City transit system. The 13-story building was designed specifically to safeguard the processing of fares, before the advent of the MetroCard. There were special security systems, a secret elevator that transported the money, and special tunnels all hidden within 370 Jay Street.

The location of the building was specifically chosen for its position above the Jay Street subway station, and tunnels were built to connect to the three subway lines – the IRT, IND, and BMT. A crashgate along the Jay Street southbound F line subway track allowed the fares to be unloaded from a special armored money train directly into the basement of the building, where the fares were taken into the tunnels and transported up several flights of stairs to an elevator that could reach the revenue room. Each subway line has its own revenue crashgate, and the Jay Street one is still visible today.

The armored money train was in operation from 1951 to 2006. Prior to this, fares were collected from the station booths and transported using armored vehicle. Six nights of the week, multiple money trains would operate at the same time picking up collections from 25 to 40 stations on each run. The two-car train held collecting agents in one car and the

revenue in the other. In 1988, 10 sets of R21 and R22 cars were converted into Money Train units.

The arrival of the MetroCard necessitated some changes in the revenue collection system, as picking up the fares from the MetroCard machines took longer than picking up a bag from the booth. The armored car system returned and revenue processing was relocated to Maspeth, Queens.

Tokens were completely phased out by 2003 and the final

trip of the Money Train took place in January 2006. The Money Room at 370 Jay Street closed the same day.

Today, you can see an example of the armored money car on display on the lower level of the New York Transit Museum in Downtown Brooklyn, and you can see the crashgate from the downtown platform of the F line at Jay Street.

Borough Hall Skyscraper Historic District

Next to Brooklyn Borough Hall, you will see signs about a Skyscraper Historic District. Ranging from 7 to 32 stories, the buildings within this historic district are far more diminutive than the domineering residential towers that have popped up a few blocks away around Jay Street-Metrotech. And they are certainly shorter than 1 Hanson Place, the Williamsburgh Savings Bank tower at Atlantic Terminal that was once the tallest building in Brooklyn. The district's name references its historical status: 21 buildings that stand as examples of the early skyscrapers in New York City. As a collection, they reflect Downtown Brooklyn's important role as a commercial hub starting after the Civil War. The construction of the Brooklyn Bridge, the expansion of the subway, and the consolidation of the boroughs increased the rate of development. Apart from being one of the less obvious historic districts – it certainly does not feel frozen in time – the Borough Hall Skyscraper Historic District is particularly unique for its wide range of architectural styles. In just a few blocks, you can find Beaux-Arts, Neoclassical, Neo-Gothic, Colonial Revival and Art Deco buildings. Look for 44 Court Street with its impressive cupolas. 32 Court Street was considered "Brooklyn's first true skyscraper" in a 1923 guidebook. 26 Court Street has a notable setback and pitched roof. The most striking of them all is 75 Livingston. Previously known as 66 Court Street, it was built as the Brooklyn Chamber of Commerce with beautiful terracotta and limestone detailing in a Neo-Gothic style. The wedding cake setbacks went "well beyond what was required by the zoning regulations and equal to that of any skyscraper in Greater New York," wrote the Landmarks Preservation Commission in 2011.

'L' BLUE AND YELLOW TILES

Loeser's department store remnants

Bond Street entrance, inside Hoyt-Schermhorn subway station
Transport: A/C/G to Hoyt-Schermerhorn

In the long hallway of the Hoyt-Schermerhorn subway station in Brooklyn, it's hard not to notice the repeated blue and yellow tiles fitted prominently with the letter 'L'. Yet, you might wonder what the

'L' signifies as there's no L train here (the A, C, and G stop here). And there's certainly no 'L' in Hoyt-Schermerhorn.

The 'L' references the Loeser's, once Brooklyn's second largest department store located on the superblock created by Fulton Street, Livingston Street, Elm Place and Bond Street. It is believed that the department store had a direct entrance to the subway and Art-Deco tiling can still be seen in the station today.

Jonathan Lenthem, author of *Motherless Brooklyn*, wrote in the essay *Speak, Hoyt-Schermerhorn* of shop display cases that once lined this same hallway. By the time he was growing up, the handsome glass cases were dusty, abandoned and broken, but they would have originally been merchandised to impress. Loeser's was copying the display cases of Abraham & Straus in the nearby Hoyt Street subway station.

The Loeser's flagship store in Downtown Brooklyn was the culmination of an enterprise founded by Frederick Loeser. The German-born entrepreneur began his business selling women's accessories and trimmings. Loeser's department store, run by Loeser and importer Howard Gibb, opened in 1887. It was wildly anticipated to "rival any of the dry goods houses for which Brooklyn is rapidly becoming noted," wrote the *Brooklyn Daily Eagle* at its opening. A million dollars of high quality merchandise was stocked inside, but buyers could expect reasonable prices in this pioneering partnership between wholesaler and retailer.

The multi-floor store was luxuriously appointed in wood, gold and bronze. It was outfitted with all the latest modern amenities: electric lighting, elevators, telephones, and floors heated by hidden steam pipes. The glove counter on the main floor was an exact replica of the one Howard Gibb saw at the Bon Marché in Paris.

Even before the shop opened, an extension was already being planned for an opening the year after. In fact, enlargements were added every one to three years until 1904. An extension constructed between 1899 and 1900 was designed by architect Frances. H. Kimball, who also designed the Montauk Club in Park Slope.

The department store closed in 1952 and the building temporarily became a J.W. May's discount store. Today, a Jennifer Convertible is in the space. The rest of the building contains offices. Over time, the building has been significantly altered: the cornices have been completely removed on the Fulton Street side and the first floors, and some façades have been drastically renovated.

The best place to take in some of the original grandeur of Loeser's is to see it from the corner of Elm Street and Livingston Street. Here you can see Kimball's extension with its arched colonnade windows and terracotta details.

ABANDONED SUBWAY STATION LEVELS

Urban explorer hotspot

Nevins Street and Bergen Street
Transport: 2/3/4/5 to Nevins Street and F/G to Bergen Street

There are a smattering of abandoned subway levels and decommissioned stations in the Downtown Brooklyn vicinity. Nevins Street was built as a station for the IRT Brooklyn line and opened in 1908. A lower level platform was intended for a connection to the Manhattan Bridge line but was never put into use. In addition, no tracks were ever laid in this level of the station and construction of the Independent Subway in the 1930s cut through it.

Nonetheless, elements of this lower level still remain. Ornamented railings on the active level lead down into an underpass with locked doors on both sides. Outside these doors is the original platform.

In 2016, artist Phil America installed a guerilla art exhibit here, accessing the site by crossing live tracks from the Hoyt Street subway station (certainly not something we recommend). As seen in photographs, the space has been so rarely accessed, it has survived all these years without a touch of graffiti. America's installation, a series of ten flags, addressed each of the mass shootings in the United States since the Columbine massacre in 1999.

Meanwhile, at Bergen Street, a station serviced by the F and G lines, a lower level was used until water damage from Smith Street led to the closure of the express platform. Silver doors on the upper level conceal open staircases that go down to the lower level. While many of the signs have been stolen by urban explorers, one key piece of signage that remains shows how Bergen was abbreviated into "Bergn".

Urban explorer @Vic.Invades described his experience down below: "The station was so cold to the point where you can see icicles frozen in time on the ceiling. You can also hear the civilians above you laughing and talking about whatever they experienced that day, while I lingered below in an empty, filthy, abandoned station. As I was down below there was a work train just sitting at the other end."

There have been some upgrades to these tracks in the last couple years and now, when the F line runs express between Jay Street and 7th Avenue, the lower level can be seen if the train is running slowly.

LONG ISLAND UNIVERSITY BASKETBALL COURT

A gym inside a historic movie theater

161 Ashland Place
Brooklyn, NY 11201
Transport: B/Q/R to DeKalb Avenue

Downtown Brooklyn, around the intersection of Flatbush Avenue and Fulton Street, was hailed as the "Times Square of Brooklyn," by the *Brooklyn Daily Eagle* in 1928. This was the year that the Paramount Theatre was under construction. The accompanying map showed 12 theaters all within a few blocks, and the *Brooklyn Daily Eagle* called it the "Hub of the Largest Theatre District in the world, excepting only New York." When the Paramount opened on November 23rd, 1928, the total combined capacity of the theaters in this area was 25,000 seats. The opening was such an important one that local businesses, such as Loeser's department store and Joe's Restaurant, took out advertisements to welcome the new venue. In addition to movies, the Paramount hosted famous performers like Ella Fitzgerald, Duke Ellington and Frank Sinatra.

Downtown Brooklyn has regained some of its entertainment cred with the arrival of the Barclays Center, the addition of BRIC Arts|Media House, and the continued excellence of the Brooklyn Academy of Music. But many of the old theaters are gone. One notable exception lies hidden inside the Long Island University Athletic Center. The basketball court sits amid an opulent backdrop, the auditorium of the former Paramount Theatre. The scoreboard sits in front of the grand stage proscenium and the original details of the theater are well preserved on the ornamented walls and arched, latticed ceiling. The Rococo flourishes get even more dramatic in the seating area thanks to the presence of large columns, fountains and sculptures. There is a custom-made Wurlitzer organ that still exists here and is operational.

The Paramount struggled financially, like other large theaters, during the Depression. It was sold in 1935 and again in 1950 to Long Island University. The original theater marquee and rooftop signage are gone, but the dramatic marble lobby now functions as the school cafeteria and an event space. Original details, like former elevators, decorative statues, various architectural elements, and private rooms, still abound within the building. You'll even find a staircase that leads to nowhere, closed off in the conversion of the space.

The gym is currently being converted back into an arts and culture venue in a joint effort by Long Island University and Brooklyn Sports and Entertainment, the management company for the Barclays Center. The venue capacity would be 1,500 – far lower than the original 4000+ when the Paramount was the largest theater in Brooklyn, but it will bring the public back into this space for the first time in over 50 years.

PRISON SHIP MARTYRS MONUMENT ⑳

Floating deathtraps

Fort Greene Park, Brooklyn
Between Cumberland Street and Myrtle and DeKalb Avenues
www.nycgovparks.org
Transport: B, D, N, Q and R trains/DeKalb Av; 2, 3, 4 and 5 trains/Nevins St; G train/Fulton St

On the forgotten subject of American prisoners of war, historian Edwin Burrows wrote: "Two obscure memorials [...] are not enough to overcome the feeling that New York City, unlike Boston or Philadelphia, has no connection whatsoever to the American Revolution." One of these memorials stands in Trinity Church; the other is a 150-foot granite column at the top of Fort Greene Park. If you're thinking that this hardly sounds obscure, ask around. Few New Yorkers have ever seen the Prison Ship Martyrs Monument; few of those who have can tell you what it's for. Add that under the column lie the remains of over 11,500 men and women, and you'll understand how mysteriously, as noted elsewhere, New York City has wiped the Revolution from its mind.

The British had a confused policy with regard to prisoners. Technically, the patriots were still British subjects and so not prisoners of war but simple traitors. Hanging would have been the ordinary punishment, but also would have poisoned any possibility of resolving the conflict with a political settlement. In the end hanging would have been a kinder result. After Washington was forced from Manhattan, British-controlled New York was a smoldering waste, a rowdy garrison for the thousands of Redcoats (by one count, over 3,000 prostitutes were brought to the city). As American prisoners began to arrive in greater numbers, the British had no plan for dealing with them. Many were crammed into sugar houses; many more filled "hulks" – ships that could float, but lacked the rigging for sailing, becoming essentially buildings on the water. More than a dozen of these hulks were anchored in the East River. On one of them alone, the HMS Jersey, over 10,000 patriots died from cold, starvation, disease, and abuse.

These prisoners of war – men and women from all thirteen colonies and a dozen countries – were given hasty burials in Wallabout Bay or simply tossed overboard. For years Brooklynites would discover dead patriots in the sand. After the war the remains were assembled and entombed near the Navy Yard. They were later moved to this permanent crypt.

Today, the only visitors allowed inside the crypt are relatives of those who perished. But on select days, such as Open House New York Weekend, the base is open to the public.

The oldest continuously run steam-powered electrical plant in the country

East Hall on Grand Avenue, between Willoughby and DeKalb Avenues
Public viewing from the balcony
Transport: G to Classon Avenue

In the middle of Clinton Hill, the 25-acre Pratt Institute campus is a gorgeous collection of landmarked buildings amidst open green space. On the first floor of East Hall (originally the Mechanical Arts

Building), in a brick building designed by William Windrim, is the Pratt Institute power generating plant. As Pratt describes, it is the "oldest continuously-operating, privately-owned, steam-powered electrical generating plant in the country," and was named a National Historical Mechanical Landmark by the American Society of Mechanical Engineers (ASME).

The steam generators currently in use were made by Ames Iron Works and installed in 1900, when a campus extension required more energy. The steam plant continues to power all of the Pratt campus, sending heat, steam and hot water to the buildings. The wood paneling in the lower Engine Room dates to 1887 and incandescent lights still illuminate the space. The building was designed with a wrap-around interior balcony for viewing. There have been notable relics added to the space, including chandeliers that were once in the Board of Directors room at the Singer Building, the tallest building in the world in 1908. ASME reports that the Chief Engineer's office has been gradually "periodized," a decor move undoubtedly by Chief Engineer Conrad Milster, an avid collector of mechanical artifacts.

Milster, a New York native, has been working at the Pratt Power Plant since 1958. Until recently, he was one of only four chief engineers in the history of Pratt Institute and sees himself as the keeper of the power plant's secrets – know-how on antiquated technologies he has garnered over the course of nearly sixty years. "Making parts is interesting, there's a sense of fulfilment," Milster said in a 2015 video interview, "It involves a lot of problem solving ... A lot of the machinery I have to deal with is obsolete, insofar as spare parts. A lot of people would say, 'Why do you have old machinery?' I have it and I like it because it's reliable."

In 2016, it was reported that Milster had been reassigned to another area in the facilities department, allegedly over controversy over his care of numerous stray cats that lived (and stayed warm) in the Engine Room. There was even once an adorable entrance just for the Pratt Cats, labeled the "Feline Staff Entrance."

It is a sad end to the career of Milster, who once said that working for a school allows him to stay true to himself: "You can be different and not be considered an oddball ... I think about retirement and I'm sort of afraid to make that move ... one of the difficulties is that when I leave, a lot of things are going to change," Milster once said. "Is anybody going to give a damn about keeping the engines nice looking? Will any modern manager put up with incandescent lighting here? Who's going to take care of the cats when I'm gone? I sort of fear for the things which I cherish being threatened." Today, you can still visit the Engine Room, but Milster is no longer there.

ABANDONED BROOKLYN NAVY YARD HOSPITAL

Hidden inside the Navy Yard

Flushing Avenue between Williamsburg Street NW and Ryerson Street
www.brooklyngreenway.org
Can be visited for occasional art exhibits and walking tours
Transport: F to York Street, G to Flushing Avenue

The Brooklyn Navy Yard Naval Hospital Annex (or the Naval Annex) was built from 1830 to 1836. It was active through the Civil War (supplying almost a third of the medicine distributed to Union soldiers) and both World Wars until it was decommissioned in the 1970s. Some of the first female nurses and medical students were employed there. Dr. E. R. Squibb, leading pharmaceutics inventor of Bristol-Myers Squibb developed the first anesthetic ethers for use in surgery here.

As it stands, however, the hospital complex has only been accessible on rare occasions. In 2015, a photographic exhibit by Bettina WitteVeen, "When We Were Soldiers ... once and young" took place inside the main building. The Brooklyn Greenway Initiative took visitors to see the hospital and surrounding areas on an annual Jane's Walk. The architecture has remained hidden behind foliage and locked gates, but has been spotted in television productions such as *Gotham*. In 2004, Steiner Studios opened as one of the first major anchor tenants of the Brooklyn Navy Yard, with five soundstages and production facilities. Starting in 2010, Steiner Studios began the process to nearly double its facility, which today is at 580,000 square feet.

In February 2015, a development plan for the third phase of expansion of Steiner Studios was adopted, with a view to converting the abandoned Brooklyn Navy Yard Hospital Annex into a media campus by 2027. With an estimated price tag of $137.1 million, the third phase would add another 420,000 square feet of floor area to the studio complex, already the largest outside of Hollywood. There will even be an underwater soundstage, the first of its kind in New York City.

The good news for preservationists is that the large-scale rehabilitation project would also include the renovation and stabilization of existing structures in the Hospital Annex.

The Brooklyn Navy Yard has been transforming from an active military property to industrial park and diversified manufacturing hub. The forthcoming arrival of a WeWork at Dock 77 and the transformation of the Navy Yard Hospital will solidify its place as one of the premiere work spaces in Brooklyn, if not New York City.

While checking out this site, don't miss the last building left from Admirals' Row further east on Flushing Avenue: a series of handsome, 19th-century townhouses that once served as officers' quarters. Another spot to see is the Naval Cemetery Landscape at 63 Williamsburg Street NW, which was reopened to the public in 2016 for the first time in 90 years.

WORLD WAR II ANTENNAS IN THE BROOKLYN NAVY YARD

23

Secret transmitter towers

25 Washington Avenue
Steiner Studios rooftop
Transport: F to York Street, G to Flushing Av

Some people think it's a bridge replica, others describe them as mini Eiffel Towers. The two structures, which have been lit up in a brilliant blue for the last few years atop Building 1 in the Brooklyn Navy Yard are actually World War II-era radio towers once used by the United States Navy.

Building 1 was the last building that remained active at the Brooklyn Navy Yard. The radio towers were operated by the Third Naval District U.S. Naval Communication Center Headquarters. In architectural plans located by Dennis Riley of the Brooklyn Navy Yard archives, you can see that the steel towers had suspension cables and a microphone trolley track running between them.

Today, they remain a source of mystery and misconception. There are claims they were used to communicate with submarines, to reach Sputnik (refuted by others), Bermuda and Puerto Rico. The latter is unlikely, especially because Puerto Rico was only within the Third Naval District from 1903 to 1919. Nonetheless, the little information that can be found about them does not reveal their actual purpose – possibly a deliberate move.

Building 1 was completed in 1942 as a material science laboratory, later known as the U.S. Naval Applied Science Laboratory. The building served as a research facility for the U.S. Navy, where electronic navigation systems for nuclear submarines were tested and refined.

The building today, run by Steiner Studios, has entered a new lease on life as part of the prolific film industry in New York City.

When Williamsburgh had an "h" in its name

Today, the neighborhood of Williamsburg is spelled without an "h" – departing from its original, more traditional spelling handed down through the English tradition.

Burghs were essentially towns created by royal charter by the King of Scotland. Williamsburgh with the "h" was incorporated as a village in 1827, though it was settled prior to this. In 1851, Williamsburgh became a city by official charter. It is believed that the "h" was dropped around 1894, when Brooklynites voted to consolidate their borough with the greater City of New York. The official consolidation of the five boroughs took place on 1 January, 1898.

Yet, you could still find street signs with the old spelling along Williamsburgh Street until a few years ago when the Federal Highway Administration mandated all road signs be changed to a combination of uppercase and lowercase letters for safety reasons. What remains, carved into grand buildings in Brooklyn, are the names of companies and organizations created before the consolidation.

One spot to track the wayward spelling is the original Williamsburgh Savings Bank at 175 Broadway, just next to the Williamsburg Bridge. The domed, Renaissance-inspired bank, built between 1870 and 1875, was recently renovated into the event space Weylin B. Seymour. However, you can still find spelling on signage all over the façade – on the two pedestals that flank the grand entrance staircase, below the pediment, and on each side of the building.

Just a few blocks away at 209 Havemeyer Street is the Dime Savings Bank of Williamsburgh, formed in 1864. It retains its original name and spelling on a frieze just below the pediment above a row of Corinthian columns. Employees still utilize the original spelling as well, even on new signage.

The Williamsburgh branch of the Brooklyn Public Library, which sits on a triangular plot at 240 Division Avenue, also preserves the original "h" on stonework above the main entrance. This building, constructed in 1903, is an example of the original "h" persisting despite an official change.

Finally, Williamsburgh with an "h" can be found even outside its own neighborhood. Look for the the metal lettering on the façade of One Hanson Place, formerly the Williamsburgh Savings Bank Tower, the tallest building in Brooklyn until 2010. Its stunning interior, once the main hall of the bank, is often used in film location shoots.

ROOFTOP REDS VINEYARD

24

The world's first commercial rooftop vineyard

Brooklyn Navy Yard
Building 275
63 Flushing Avenue
Brooklyn, NY 11249
703-582-8609
www.rooftopreds.com
Hours vary, check website
Exclusive tours and wine tasting with Rooftop Reds founders take place through
Untapped Cities every weekend May to September – age restriction 21+
Transport: F to York Street, G to Flushing Avenue

Hidden within the Brooklyn Navy Yard, Rooftop Reds vineyard was founded by Devin Shomaker, his brother Thomas Shomaker, and Chris Papalia. It is the world's first commercially viable rooftop vineyard.

Devin Shomaker worked as an entrepreneur before going to graduate school for winemaking in the Finger Lakes of New York State. He tailored his classes there towards the creation of a rooftop vineyard, often finding himself at odds with the traditional winemakers who were his teachers.

Undeterred, the team got started on the roof of Thomas's Brooklyn apartment with a pilot of 50 vines in 2013. The Brooklyn Navy Yard gave Rooftop Reds space to start the endeavor on the rooftop of building 292 in May of 2014, and in 2015, the vines were transferred to Building 275.

As Devin explains, the rooftop's location and wind pattern is ideal for wine growing. On the rooftop of Building 275 is a reflective white membrane that reduces surface heat temperature and reflects light back into the canopy to increase photosynthetic activity – a viticulture advantage specific to this cultivation, and the primary reason the Rooftop Reds team chose the building.

Within the 14,800 square foot space, the vineyard has 50 custom urban planter systems that Rooftop Reds developed with Cornell University and Finger Lakes industry leaders. Five Bordeaux varietals are being grown: Malbec, Cabernet Sauvignon, Cabernet Franc, Petit Verdot and Merlot. European cuttings have been grafted to American rootstock, fused together in a year long process in a grape vine nursery.

Because the vines were transferred to the Navy Yard, the team is giving the crop the full, recommended time for cultivation. The first harvest took place in 2017, their fourth growing season, and Rooftop Reds is open for tastings of the Finger Lakes-grown wines under its label. The wines grown on the Brooklyn Navy Yard rooftop will be aged and bottled up in the Finger Lakes. The rooftop also has a tasting room, a lounge area with hammocks and turf, and a great view.

When asked whether Shomaker will license the technology, he says that for now, he just wants to encourage the urban agriculture movement. He hopes to expand Rooftop Reds to other cities. "We need greener cities," Devin says.

25

FARM INSIDE DOMINO SUGAR FACTORY SITE

Hidden waterfront farm to table spot

320 Kent Avenue
Brooklyn, NY 11249
www.northbrooklynfarms.com
Tuesday–Sunday 11am–8pm
Transport: F to York Street, G to Flushing Avenue

Inside the construction zone at the Domino Sugar Factory redevelopment site on the Williamsburg waterfront is an organic farm that exists due to a special community partnership between the developer, Two Trees Management Company, and the neighborhood.

Formerly located in a vacant lot across the street from the Domino plot, North Brooklyn Farms moved to be directly along the waterfront in May of 2015. Beneath the imposing structure of the former sugar refinery building grow flowers and produce, sold through a weekly Community Shared Agriculture program. A shipping container is used as a mushroom farm. The food grown here, cultivated and cared for by volunteers, is also used for events and dinners hosted on site. How's that for farm to table? From the picnic tables, you can literally reach over into the produce beds.

But mostly, this is a green public space for the community and a welcome respite from the flurry of construction and development in Williamsburg. There are rounded grass craters that function as "seats for humans" along the edge of the space and there's also a state-of-the-art outdoor skate park.

When the original location closed, neighborhood children were visibly upset, waiting at the entrance of the formerly empty lot, which is now another Williamsburg development. Two Trees worked with North Brooklyn Farm and Ride Brooklyn to relocate the farm onto the Domino property itself, opening this portion of the waterfront up to the public for the first time in 150 years.

Almost none of this can be seen behind the barricades of the construction site, but it's a true jewel of a spot most people miss on a visit to Williamsburg, and a great place to take in views of the East River, Manhattan, and the Williamsburg Bridge.

Anybody can volunteer to work here, just sign up on the North Brooklyn Farms website. They have two volunteer days a week, one on weekdays and one on the weekend. You have to be at least 18 years old, but the farm encourages urbanites to come and get their hands dirty. Volunteer activities also include event planning, and giving farm tours. North Brooklyn Farms also hosts private events.

26

THE CITY RELIQUARY

The minutiae of the metropolis

370 Metropolitan Avenue, Brooklyn
www.cityreliquary.org
718-782-4842
Weekends 12pm–6pm
Transport: L train/Bedford Av; G train/Metropolitan Av

You may not know yet that you're interested in scale models of the Statue of Liberty, or the skeletons of urban rats, or rock samples from the different New York boroughs. But you probably are. Helping you realize this is what The City Reliquary in Williamsburg is about.

The museum is small, and started smaller: in early days it was just a street-level window display in a private apartment. Now the nonprofit spreads over three rooms in its current space on Metropolitan Avenue. There is a feeling of fragility and time here, like the contents of an old forgotten suitcase. The title "reliquary" is apt: the museum contains physical remains of New York City – but not the major ones. Here you'll find instead the lost minutiae that lived in the margins.

"We use display to tell a story about an object," current president Bill Scanga summarizes. "These, for example," showing an array of old brass subway tokens. "We're not using tokens anymore, but you put them under glass and it changes your perception of this thing you had in your pocket: it creates this sense of value." In the center of the main room fragments of buildings – old rubble, essentially – are arrayed to suggest statuary. Mounted high on the wall like the heads of hunted game are hand straps from the city buses and subways. One cabinet purports to gloss New York geology: if you've always wanted to compare samples of Bronx dirt and Brooklyn dirt, here's your opportunity. A dusty old hammer bears the tag: "Old Hammer."

One display expresses the museum perhaps better than any other. Arrayed like ancient vases on a shelf is an extensive collection tagged "Seltzer Bottles of Brooklyn." It seems at least partly tongue-in-cheek: the seltzer bottle is, after all, the stuff of slapstick gags. But the gags are yesterday's gags. Looking at the bottles all together, with their various colors and manufacturing marks, is to connect with a lost way of doing things, to pass your eyes over the finer texture of the city's history.

NORTH BROOKLYN BOAT CLUB

Inviting and gritty

Entrance: 49 Ash Street at McGuinness Boulevard, Brooklyn
www.northbrooklynboatclub.org
Membership dues: $40/year
Regular free paddles in kayaks and canoes as well as other events; check website
for schedule
Transport: 7 train/Vernon Blvd – Jackson Av; G train/Greenpoint Av

For a general sense of what it's about, the best way to approach the North Brooklyn Boat Club is walking over the Pulaski Bridge from Queens. The feeling is: this is a landscape where urbanity won. Rail yards, tollbooths, tunnels, every kind of concrete, steel stanchions and trusses, fences topped with barbed wire. Then, down below on the Greenpoint side of Newtown Creek, you see a well-tended strip of alley that leads to a floating platform and, scattered in the dark water around it, brightly colored kayaks.

The club, which has nearly 200 paying members, keeps its boats in corrugated shipping containers, that emblem of reclaimed design, and you get to it through an entrance cloaked in morning glories and banked by a neat garden bed full of butternut squash. It didn't get this way by itself. "This was covered in weeds, and just junk, and old trucks," says Scott Behr, a club member whose metal shop is down the street. "I kept seeing it get cleaned up, so I just came down here one day and was like: What are you guys *doing*? And they said: It's a boat club!"

In the city you can take a canoe down an idyllic river, or among islets in a bay: here you row to discover the dirty, enveloping, magnificent city. Inland is New York's main water treatment facility and the still waters of Newtown Creek, which is more off-putting either for the millions of gallons of oil spilled there over the years, or for the raw muck that flows into it from the city's sewers—hard to say. West lies the fast and wild tidal estuary of the East River and the iconic skyline. Figuring out your place among these forces is part of getting out in this water. Members take off alone; visitors paddle in groups. Watching Manhattan grow slowly larger as massive barges slide past the unpretty face of the industrial shorefront, and hard-ass tugboat workers grin and raise their gloved thumb at you, you'll feel connected to the city's very guts.

In the afternoon, founding member Fung Lim starts a fire in the club's brick pit and makes popcorn in a stock pot. Lanky and smiling, with a black ponytail and the hands of somebody who knows his way around a toolbox, Lim has helped form the club's unique vibe: inviting and gritty. "It's not a Sunday picnic paddle on a nice calm lake," he says. "But people have to use something and appreciate it and have fun on it before they can say: this is mine. That's where we come in."

TOUR OF THE NEWTOWN CREEK DIGESTER EGGS

Futuristic sewage treatment plant with two honors for Excellence in Design

327 Greenpoint Avenue
Brooklyn, NY 11222
718-595-5140
Visitor Center open by appointment only
Tours through advance registration only
Transport: G to Greenpoint Avenue

On special occasions, such as Valentine's Day and Halloween, the New York City Department of Sanitation hosts tours of the Newtown Creek Wastewater Treatment Plant, the largest of the city's 14 facilities. As unromantic or unfestive as a sewage treatment plant might sound, tickets for these free tours are snapped up so fast there's often a long wait list. The Newtown Creek facility has become something of a city landmark, with its eight 140-foot metallic silver digester eggs that rise from the banks of Newtown Creek, an industrial zone at the border of Brooklyn and Queens. At night, the eggs glow with a deep blue color, part of an overall scheme by lighting designer Hervé Descottes.

This shiny facility, which opened in 2010, was designed by Polshek Partners, now Ennead Architects, the firm behind renovations at Carnegie Hall, Brooklyn Museum and the American Museum of Natural History. Ennead also designed the Standard Hotel in the Meatpacking District. The Newtown Creek project was a collaboration between the community, the architects and the New York City Department of Sanitation, and is upheld as an example of collective planning at its best. As a testament, the New York City Arts Commission awarded the Newtown Creek Wastewater Treatment Plant with two honors for Excellence in Design.

New York City has a combined sewer system, which means stormwater, wastewater and sewage flow in the same pipes. During storms and heavy rains, the system gets overwhelmed and sewage gets discharged directly into rivers and bays. The digester eggs, however, process between 1.3 to 1.5 billion gallons of sludge a day in a multi-step process that eventually helps reduce the amount of sewage that flows into the city's waterways. The sludge is heated up, reducing its oxygen content, which allows bacteria to break down the waste into water, carbon dioxide and methane. Water is removed from the "digested sludge" which becomes a solid that can be used as fertilizer. The remaining liquid is then disinfected with enough oxygen to still support marine life.

The New York City waterways are the cleanest they've been in 100 years, and the Newtown Creek plant is a big reason for that.

Tours begin in the visitors' center before heading up an elevator to the glass walkways that run between the digester eggs. You can peer down into the sludge and see the process at work while taking in the views of Manhattan and Brooklyn.

KINGSLAND WILDFLOWERS
GREEN ROOF AT BROADWAY STAGES

A hidden green oasis atop an oil spill zone

520 Kingsland Avenue
Brooklyn, NY 11222
Transport G subway to Greenpoint Ave
http://www.kingslandwildflowers.com/
Open seasonally April-November for educational programming, special events,
or book a tour through the website

At the northeastern tip of Greenpoint, the former facilities of Standard Oil once encompassed 50 acres of former marshland along Newtown Creek. That industrial landscape persists today – active oil and fuel storage sites, the remnants of those long gone, and new industry – despite encroaching gentrification. Several decades of mishandling resulted in a century of accumulated oil contamination and a fire in 1919 causing a loss of 110 million gallons of oil. Today we see extensive pollution of the Newtown Creek waterway in addition to an estimated 17 to 30 million gallons of crude oil resting just below the surface of fifty acres of land underneath Greenpoint, Brooklyn.

In compliance with the Sherman Antitrust Act of 1914, Standard Oil was divided into six companies, and those resulting companies are still some of the biggest players globally today. ExxonMobil is just one, and still operates here in Greenpoint. As part of a petroleum remediation agreement with New York State, ExxonMobil has been extracting oil from the ground from the many spills and fires that have roared through the refineries and oil plants over the last 150 years.

But amidst the foreboding landscape, glimpses of nature can still be found. One such place is Kingsland Wildflowers, a lush series of green roofs hidden atop Broadway Stages, one of the largest TV and film production companies in New York City. Funded predominantly by the Greenpoint Community Environmental Fund, a grant program created from the ExxonMobil settlement, and Broadway Stages, KingslandWildflowers was conceived by Marni Marjorelle, the owner and founder of Alive Structures green roofing company, in partnership with NYC Audubon and Newtown Creek Alliance. In addition to monitoring wildlife populations on the green roofs, New York City Audubon and Newtown Creek Alliance run the community programming: hosting special events, workshops, neighborhood bird walks, ecology discussions, and educational lectures.

In total, there are four green roofs, all donated by Broadway Stages, covering 22,000 square feet with a fifth roof on the way that will serve as a living learning lab and educational green roof. Kingsland Wildflowers aims to offer a habitat of native grasses and wildflowers for the birds and insects of the neighborhood, some who live their whole lives on this roof, others that use the roof as a stopover habitat. The rooftop oasis has become a hotspot for bird species like the barn swallow, red-tailed hawk, and chimney swift, European starling, northern mockingbird, and the American robin. From May through October 2017, New York City Audubon collected over 45,000 arthropods, observed 17 bird species, recorded 493 bat passes, and confirmed one species of bat, the Eastern Red Bat.

Stunning views

The views, with a backdrop of the Newtown Creek Digester Eggs (see page 64) and the New York City skyline, are stunning. On the fifth floor green roof, a meandering stone path leads to a spherical water fountain that seems to be in dialogue with the otherworldly digester eggs. It's a reminder that Kingsland Wildflowers is not a naturally occurring Garden of Eden, but that nature can be found even in the most inhospitable of places.

30

BROOKLYN TAXIDERMY CLASSES ㉚

"Please do not feed the animals. They're stuffed"

681 Morgan Avenue
Brooklyn, NY 11222
www.brooklyntaxidermy.com
By appointment only
Transport: G subway to Nassau Avenue

On the second floor of a brick warehouse building, next to a metal fabrication shop on a Greenpoint street, an unmarked taxidermy studio is run by entomology artist Amber Maykut. "Please do not feed the animals. They're stuffed" reads a humorous sign on the wall inside the Brooklyn Taxidermy studio.

A peacock, replete with feathers, perches on a branch surrounded by a wall of antlers. Deer, a bear, a raccoon and a wolf keep watch, along with smaller birds, squirrels, mice and butterflies. In one corner sits Maykut's workbench, with a wall of her tools of the trade. A central table is used for classes.

Maykut was originally a self-taught taxidermist, learning the trade as a hobby while working as a corporate writer and editor. After downsizing to a smaller apartment, Maykut, a self-proclaimed hoarder and collector, decided to sell some of her work online and unexpectedly discovered her pieces were in high demand, even causing bidding wars.

She took the plunge and began studying taxidermy formally at several schools in the New York and New Jersey area, learning from notable artists in the industry on the way to receiving her certification in bird and mammal taxidermy. She interned at the American Museum of Natural History, working on the dioramas within the special exhibitions and fabrication department. And she was the taxidermist-in-residence and teacher at the now defunct Morbid Anatomy Museum. Anybody who has visited the museum will have seen her work, which was on display throughout the two floors, including a memorable work featuring white squirrels in a convertible. Maykut has been featured in the New York Times, VICE Magazine, The Guardian, National Geographic, and on the Discovery Channel.

When the museum closed, she set up the Greenpoint studio where she now works and teaches classes. She also works as an artist and fabricator for the Evolution Store in Manhattan and sells her work on Etsy. Most of her students are women in their twenties. Maykut says, "It's a new demographic of young people in an urban setting that dig the small, whimsical, cabinet of curiosities style of taxidermy." Even so, her students come from a wide cross section of the city and the world — from children to couples on dates, and even a Hasidic Jewish couple who are regular clients. "It's New York City, you're going to get every walk of life you can imagine," she says.

BROOKLYN GRANGE

31

A rooftop soil farm 100 feet up

Brooklyn Navy Yard Building #3
63 Flushing Avenue, Brooklyn, NY 11205
Transport: F train to York Street; buses B67, B48, B57, B62, B69

Brooklyn Grange, with two rooftops in New York City, is the world's largest rooftop soil farm. The Brooklyn location is in Building 3 at the Brooklyn Navy Yard; the original Long Island City location opened in 2010. The farm cultivates over 50,000 pounds of organic produce a year. It also operates a chicken coop and an apiary with over 30 honey bee hives on roofs across the city. The produce is sold to restaurants as well as to the public through community shared agriculture programs and a weekly farm stand where you can buy tomatoes, lettuce, kale, peppers, ground cherries, garlic, and wildflowers. It's not a gimmick; the aerial fields are sustainable and even profitable. Rooftop farms work, and Brooklyn Grange was the early pioneer in New York City.

"We use this mixture called Rooflite," says Bradley, the farm manager, scooping up a handful of earth specked with flinty rock. "It's a good growing medium because it's got these porous stones." Not that weight is an issue; the industrial roof, which was specially prepared with layers of absorbent felt and runoff collecting measures, could withstand four times as much. The soil is enriched with compost; the farm creates its own with a solar-powered system. You can see how this works yourself on any Saturday during the growing season (Spring to Fall). And aside from the peculiar charm of taking an elevator to a tended field, you'll find it worth visiting for the view. The Manhattan skyline dominates the horizon; the city grid and the orderly rows of vegetables turn out to be a natural match.

While you're stooped over weeding or picking turnips you might forget that you're 100 feet up. "It's funny, yeah," says Bradley, motioning towards a glittering cityscape. "Oftentimes I don't look at this all day. Then, I love it when everybody goes home at the end of the day and I have time to myself with the plants and check out the view as the sun goes down."

In addition to a diverse range of workshops for the public, Brooklyn Grange also works with a local non-profit partner, City Growers, and hosts 17,000 New York City youths every year for tours and workshops.

THE MYSTERY
OF ARBITRATION ROCK

A disputed boundary marker

Onderdonk House
1820 Flushing Avenue
Ridgewood, NY 11385
718-456-1775
ridgewoodhistoricalsociety@gmail.com
Saturday 1pm–5pm

32

In 1769, a large glacial boulder was used to mark the boundary between Kings County and Queens County in an attempt to end a century-old border dispute between the towns of Bushwick and Newtown. "Arbitration Rock" served as a boundary marker until the 1920s or 30s, when the rock is assumed to have been buried underground during the extension of Onderdonk Avenue.

Thought to have been dynamited to bits or lost to time, Arbitration Rock was found and excavated through a seven-year quest by William Asadorian, a librarian with the New York Public Library. Researching archival maps and documents, Asadorian was confident he knew where the rock lay. As utility work was already in the pipeline, the City of New York agreed to do the dig... and brought up the rock.

It was placed in the backyard of the Onderdonk House, a Dutch stone house that is a New York City, State and federal landmark, along the original boundary between Brooklyn and Queens (in 1925, the borough maps were redrawn because the original boundary line was running through the middle of people's homes).

Despite what seems to be a definitive discovery, Arbitration Rock continues to be a source of debate. Some believe it's the wrong rock entirely. Others are upset that it was moved to this location at the Onderdonk House, which effectively means it belongs to Queens. The Director of the Greater Astoria Historical Society believes Arbitration Rock may be an entirely different boulder all together, located in front of a fence on Varick Avenue, about five blocks away.

Regardless, Arbitration Rock seems comfortable in its current home, surrounded by a white picket fence and celebrated with a new plaque.

NEARBY

Oko Farms

(33)

104 Moore Street – Brooklyn, NY 11206
www.okofarms.com
Guided tours available
Transport: J/M subway to Lorimer Street, or L to Montrose Avenue

Situated between a liquor store and a smoke shop on the Williamsburg/Bushwick border, Oko Farms is New York City's oldest and only outdoor aquaponics farm. But very little on the street indicates its existence, although the curious may be intrigued by the NYC Parks Department Greenthumb sign and a tattered laminated diagram – the only indicators that something is growing within.

Aquaponic farming combines hydroponics with aquaculture, utilizing a closed cycle that repurposes the nutrient-rich excreta of fish as fertilizer. The plants then filter the toxic waste and provide clean water back to the fish.

MAGNOLIA GRANDIFLORA

*One of only two trees designated
as New York City landmarks*

679 Lafayette Avenue
Brooklyn, NY 11216
www.magnoliatreeearthcenter.com
Transport: G to Bedford/Nostrand Avenues

A magnolia tree on Lafayette avenue, between Marcy and Tompkins Avenues in Bedford-Stuyvesant, is one of only two trees that have been designated as New York City landmarks. This tree, of the species Magnolia grandiflora, was planted in 1885 by William Lemken from a seedling brought back from North Carolina. Placed in front of his townhouse, the evergreen tree releases white lemon-scented flowers which are the state flowers of Mississippi and Louisiana. The species hails from North Carolina, and was one of the first exotic trees to be exported to Europe. It can grow up to 70 feet tall, but rarely survives north of Philadelphia.

This particular tree was designated a New York City landmark on February 3rd, 1970 by a unanimous vote. In a public hearing, however, opinions were more mixed – nine spoke in favor, eight were opposed. Regardless, the Landmarks Preservation Commission clearly felt passionate about the tree, writing in the official designation report, "It is all the more remarkable, therefore, that the seedling which Mr. William Lemken sent up from North Carolina some 85 years ago ... should have survived so long. It is thus for its inherent beauty as well as for its rare hardiness that this particular Magnolia grandiflora has become a neighborhood symbol and a focus of community pride."

In fact, local resident Hattie Carthan was responsible for the preservation of the tree in the 1950s and raised funds for it in the face of oncoming development. A parking lot and housing projects were planned just next to it. Carthan founded the Magnolia Tree Earth Center in 1972 to bring green programs to the Bedford-Stuyvesant neighborhood, using the symbol of the famous tree to encourage environmental awareness and youth development in the community. The Magnolia Tree Earth Center is still active today, located next door at 677 Lafayette Street.

Unlike other landmark designation reports, the one for Magnolia grandiflora contained very specific instructions due to its unique nature. These specifications included how buildings on the block were to be demolished in order to protect the tree from new construction, what thermostat settings needed to be in new basement rooms, and how to care for the ground around the tree. "The Commission, no more than any of the ardent proponents of this designation, wishes to see a dead tree as a Landmark," they wrote.

Sadly, scaffolding has been up on the brownstone at 679 Lafayette Avenue since 2011 ... but the Magnolia tree is still standing tall.

BROWNSTONE JAZZ

1930s throwback

107 Macon Street
Brooklyn, NY 11216
www.sankofaaban.com
Facebook page: BrownstoneJAZZ@Sankofa Aban BnB
Transport: A/C to Nostrand Avenue

There's a lot happening in Bedford-Stuyvesant these days. In one of the stately brownstones for which the neighborhood is known, the Sankofa Aban Bed and Breakfast hosts weekend jazz concerts on the parlor floor. The evenings evoke an earlier era, when the number of jazz clubs in this outer borough was equal to those in Manhattan. Jazz greats like Miles Davis, Thelonius Monk and Max Roach performed here. The Brownstone JAZZ concerts and the rich historical tradition they reference are important for this community – one that has weathered the gang wars and racial riots of the 1960s to 1980s, along with the rapacious gentrification of the last decade.

More than just a place for local talent to bubble up, Brownstone JAZZ has also brought jazz notables to Bed-Stuy. The concerts are curated by Blue Note recording bassist Eric Lemon, who has invited musicians like James Spaulding, Kiane Zawadi, and Broadway singer Bonacella Lewis to perform on a regular basis. Like the jazz sessions of yesteryear, there's a sense of the collective here – their home is your home, at least for an evening. Anybody can take up an instrument in jam sessions and the audience often breaks into song. "Remember When," is the motto.

Brownstone JAZZ co-founder Debbie McClain happened upon this vocation by accident. McClain comes from six generations of music enthusiasts and once studied the piano. She trained as a hairdresser and never dreamed of owning a bed and breakfast. But her grandparents' brownstone "fell into her lap to save and maintain," she says, and she knew that "music would cleanse this 19th century home."

The parlor room and guest rooms have wonderful antique details that lend to the experience of Bronwstone JAZZ. Victorian woodwork and stained glass windows create a substantial stage-like setting for the performers. Three impressive custom wooden cabinets line the parlor room and create a substantial stage-like setting for the performers. Guests mingle on the parquet floors, in front of mirrored fireplace mantels.

To seal the deal, included in the cover charge is a Southern-style fish fry with sides of cornbread and coleslaw. The profits go to the musicians and to fund free music workshops held at Sankofa Aban during the week.

The best way to keep tabs with the schedule is to follow the organization on Facebook at the page called "BrownstoneJAZZ@ Sankofa Aban BnB."

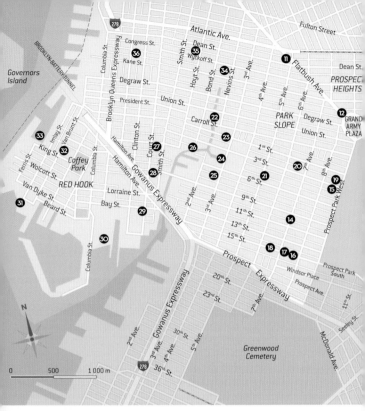

Brownstone belt and beyond

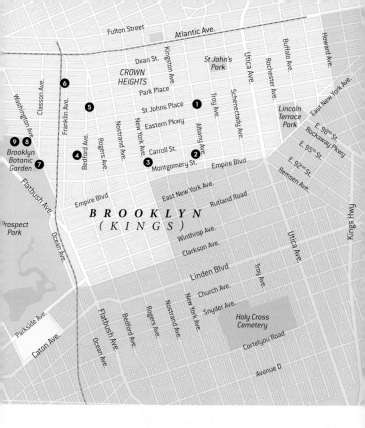

770 EASTERN PARKWAY

The holiest place on earth

*Chabad-Lubavitch World
Headquarters, Brooklyn
718-774-4000
www.chabad.org
See jewishtours.com for tickets and tours*

Number 770 Eastern Parkway in the Crown Heights neighborhood of Brooklyn is the world headquarters of the Chabad movement of Orthodox Judaism, commonly called Lubavitch. The house on Eastern Parkway was purchased in 1940 to be the workplace, home, yeshivah, and synagogue of the sixth Lubavitcher Rebbe, Rabbi Yosef Yitzchak Schneersohn, who escaped from Nazi-occupied Warsaw to New York. The site is the holiest place on Earth among Lubavitchers; they call it simply "770". It has doubles in more than a dozen places around the world, and is an example of a building with such a strong symbolic hold that followers of this religious group have replicated it as they've spread. The original building was also once the workplace of Grand Rebbe Menachem Mendel Schneerson.

Number 770 and the adjacent seminary are open to the curious, a surprise that guide Rabbi Beryl Epstein (who has unfortunately passed since the last edition of *Secret New York*, from where this entry was adapted) seemed to enjoy delivering.

"Look around," he smiles. "Take pictures, whatever you want." He pointed out a rare 19th century lunar clock and a row of wooden lecterns, arranged chronologically, that the rabbi used during his stewardship. Particularly interesting are the books on the Kabbalah once owned by Rabbi Yosef Yitzchak Schneersohn, who brought the movement to the United States and announced his successor's messiahship. The margins of the books are filled with scrawls in red and purple; Schneersohn was under arrest in Russia when he wrote them and had only berries to use for ink. Lubavitchers have spent lifetimes interpreting these annotations. "This is not Madonna's Kabbalah," Epstein chuckled. "It's the real thing."

The seminary next door has a gallery where, through tinted glass, visitors can witness living scholarship: thousands of rabbinical students debating scripture. It's a storm of activity, a little like the floor of a stock exchange. The room is so tightly packed, the young men walk across tables to get from one group to another. On the street, a visiting Lubavitcher from Israel explained how you can tell if a Hasid belongs to the sect: his hat will have a pinched crown and the brim pulled down. He straightens his own battered fedora with a self-mocking frown. "A couple of hours in 770 and let's see what your hat looks like."

SUKKHOT

Dancing deep in Hasidic territory

Kingston Avenue and Crown Street
Takes place mid-Tishrei; see calendar: www.hebcal.com
Transport: 3 train/Kingston Av

Try this: during the week-long holiday of Sukkot, on any night except Shabbat (Friday), take the 3 train to Eastern Parkway and walk down Kingston Avenue. With every step, you're getting deeper into the world of Hasidic New York, a close-knit community governed by ancient customs. Within this rigid structure, it makes good sense that a time is set aside for society to completely let loose; "Simchat beit hashoeva" is it.

As you head down the avenue, you'll be aware of a buzz in the street: men in black hats and suits rushing south, teams of kids leaping along the sidewalks while their mothers bring up the rear. When you hit Carroll Street it's clear that something festive is underway; the trees are swept by the red and blue lights of parked police cars, on a stage, bearded men shred klezmer music on electric guitars, and the street has become a barricaded gully. The heart of the dance party is at Kingston and Crown.

Enter this area (men only), and you'll likely get sucked into the current. "Take pictures later. Now is dancing," shouts one reveler, slapping his fedora on your correspondent's head and dragging him into the melee. The women watch from the sidewalks, silhouetted by the glow of dime stores and restaurants, many of which will stay open all night. Aside from the custom of separated sexes, the feel is small-town county fair: cotton candy, popcorn, canned cola. If there were room for a Tilt-A-Whirl on Kingston, there'd be one.

Among the Hasidim, Lubavitchers are known to reach out. "Chabad Lubavitch's mission is to be a light unto the world," says Nachman, a young married man. "We're trained to interact with people in general." Lubavitchers believe that their Rebbe Menachem Schneerson (who lived only a couple of blocks away) was the Messiah of prophecy. This is why you'll get away with crashing the party – the more people, the more light gets spread.

BELGIAN BLOCK STREET FROM THE BATTLE OF BROOKLYN

Forgotten Revolutionary road

Clove Road between Empire Boulevard and Montgomery Street
Transport: 2/5 to President Street

I n the midst of the street grid in Crown Heights is an odd diagonal mid-block street known as Clove Road. Located behind an A&P supermarket, it's so forgotten that the Google Street View car didn't even bother to turn down it. Yet, it may have one of the richest and longest histories of any street in the neighborhood.

Clove Road is what remains of a Native American trail and later Colonial era road, retaining some of its old Belgian blocks* to boot. Architect Michael Cetera, who has studied Clove Road in depth, says it was also an important location in the American Revolutionary War and was one of the first roads in Brooklyn to be paved. It was also possibly a portion of, or nearby, the Bedford Pass, which allowed passage through a ridge that is today's Eastern Parkway. American troops used this pass to retreat back to Brooklyn Heights during the Battle of Brooklyn.

Rectangular pieces of granite that came from ship ballast, the Belgian block is commonly miswritten as cobblestone. The two are actually different.

The name "Clove" comes from the Dutch *kleft*, meaning a cleft between two hills that have since been flattened. Clove Road was originally much longer, running from present day Fulton Street to Empire Boulevard, after which it was known as Canarsie Avenue. As Kevin Walsh from *Forgotten New York* explains, it was perhaps intended that Clove Road would be eliminated when the new street grid was laid out, but this section, between Montgomery Street and Empire Boulevard, somehow lingered on.

Cetera hopes to commemorate the rich history of the road through the placement of a 7-foot-story stone, carved by artist Kenichi Hiratsuka. Hiratsuka's work would tell the road's early history pictorially using his signature chiseled line technique. "Everything I do, I carve one continuous line that never cross each other. It's almost like carving a tattoo on the stone," he said in 2014. The project was approved by the local community board, but has faltered while awaiting approvals from the city's Design Commission.

Malbone street wreck: deadliest train crash in NYC subway history

In 1918, a train wreck on Malbone Street was so infamous that the entire thoroughfare was renamed Empire Boulevard. At least 93 people lost their lives, with an additional hundred or so injured, when a wooden five-car Brooklyn Rapid Transit (BRT) train derailed. It all began with a motorman strike, which started earlier that day on 1 November, 1918. Despite a lack of trained operators, the BRT went ahead with service anyway forcing an inexperienced dispatcher to take the reins of this particular train. The curve towards the Prospect Park Subway Station was meant to be taken at six miles per hour, but the train was estimated to have been going at 30 to 40 miles per hour (a Naval officer on the train thought it was over 70). The first train car fell into a concrete partition between the north and southbound tracks, with the following cars cutting through and disintegrating it. There were no survivors at all in the first car. The BRT went into bankruptcy less than two months later, re-emerging as the Brooklyn Manhattan Transit Company (BMT).

Today, you can find one small street (half a block long) that is still called Malbone Street. Forgotten in the renaming, it's located just off of Clove Road, between Nostrand and New York avenues just north of Empire Boulevard. The Malbone Street tunnel also still exists on the Franklin Avenue shuttle line. The tunnel is located at the edge of Prospect Park, beneath the intersection of Empire Boulevard, Flatbush Avenue and Ocean Avenue.

FORMER EBBETS FIELD SITE
OF THE BROOKLYN DODGERS

An iconic baseball site

1720 Bedford Ave
Brooklyn, NY 11225
Transport: B/Q/S Prospect Park Subway or 2/3 to President Street

The Los Angeles Dodgers have an origin story firmly planted in Brooklyn, although there is tragically not much left to see. In the early years of baseball, most teams were usually referred to simply by their uniform colors. Newspapers reporting on the burgeoning sport provided nicknames, which often changed.

The early Dodgers team, known under such names as the Brooklyn Atlantics, the Bridgerooms, the Superbas and others, practiced at the

first Washington Park, around the Old Stone House in Park Slope. After moving to the second Washington Park in Gowanus in 1898, the Dodgers then moved to Ebbets Field in Crown Heights, Brooklyn.

Ground broke on Ebbets Field in 1912 and the stadium opened in 1913. The stadium had an Italian marble rotunda, inside which hung a chandelier made of baseballs and bats. Here, the Brooklyn Dodgers would win their only World Series title, over the New York Yankees in 1955. Ebbets Field is also where Jackie Robinson, the first African American baseball player in major league baseball, played for the Dodgers. It was soon clear, however, that Ebbets Field was too small for the Dodgers fan base. Team owner Walter O'Malley hoped to build a new, larger stadium at Atlantic Yards, where the Barclays Center stands today, but New York City master builder Robert Moses had grand plans for Flushing Meadows-Corona Park, site of the 1939 and 1964 World's Fairs. Refusing to move the team to Queens, O'Malley looked into using Los Angeles as a leveraging tool against Moses but ended up taking the offer to move cities. Ebbets Field closed in 1957 and was demolished in 1960.

Today, a hulking 24-story housing project stands in its place. Its name, Ebbets Field Apartments, is one of the few reminders of its illustrious baseball history. Tragically, a sign reads "No ball playing."

Behind a bush, under the building's address number, is a cornerstone inscribed with the words "This is the former site of Ebbets Field." The year 1962 is shown inside a baseball to mark the year the apartments were constructed.

In a parking lot just off Sullivan Place, a forgotten plaque on the sidewalk marks the original location of the Ebbets Field home plate.

The origin of the Dodgers' name

The Dodgers' name comes from the literal dodging of Brooklyn's trolleys by the borough's residents, as crossing the city's streets amidst the new transportation method was a deadly sport in itself. In fact, the team was originally known as the Brooklyn Trolley Dodgers. It should also be noted that there are some who believe the term comes from Brooklynites evading or "dodging" the farebox, but the official Dodgers history matches the traffic reference. It wasn't until 1933 that the team put the word Dodgers on their uniforms.

Other small tributes to the baseball team are nearby: PS 375 Jackie Robinson School and Jackie Robinson playground are just behind the apartment building. A Jehovah's Witness church two blocks away calls itself the Ebbets Field Congregation.

REMNANTS OF AUTOMOBILE ROW

What's left of a bygone auto industry

Bedford Avenue between Empire Boulevard and Fulton Street
Transport: 2/3/4/5 to Franklin Avenue

By the early 1900s, Brooklyn was bustling and its wealthy residents were participating in the automobile craze with a fervor equal to their Manhattan counterparts. Much of the automobile industry was

clustered in Crown Heights along Bedford Avenue, the longest street in Brooklyn and a key north-south thoroughfare in the borough. Bedford Avenue was also in close proximity to Brooklyn's cultural institutions, like the Brooklyn Museum and Prospect Park, and to wealthy residents living in the mansions of Crown Heights and the pre-war apartments on Eastern Parkway, Brooklyn's answer to Paris' Champs-Élysées.

From 1911 through World War II, The Brooklyn Auto Show was hosted in the great drill hall of the 23rd Regiment Armory, at the corner of Bedford Avenue and Atlantic Avenue. A 1912 business directory includes 25 automobile-related companies on Bedford Avenue alone between Empire Boulevard and Fulton Street. The construction of Ebbets Field (the Brooklyn Dodgers' stadium) in 1913 along Bedford Avenue brought more traffic and consumers to the area.

Although there remains a clustering of auto repair shops in Crown Heights, it is far from how Brooklyn's Automobile Row felt in its heyday, when the major automobile brands – Ford, Chrysler, Buick, General Motors, Pontiac – were sold in dealerships and showrooms along Bedford Avenue, with service centers and garages rounding out the auto-related offerings.

The Depression, suburbanization and World War II spelled the end of Automobile Row, but if you look closely, many of the buildings still stand. And if you look up, you'll catch some beautiful ornamentation on the façades, sometimes related to the auto industry.

Notable spots south of Eastern Parkway include the Firestone service station on Empire Boulevard, with a fantastic Art Deco-era overhang, and the Simons Motor Sales Co. repair shop at 1590 Bedford Avenue across from the Bedford-Union Armory. The Simons showroom was further north at 1425 Bedford Avenue, a one-floor building that still stands. At the corner of Eastern Parkway, the building that now houses the W.E.B. DuBois High School still has signs of its former use – outlines of first floor garages, into which an entrance has been built. Across Eastern Parkway, a Chase Bank occupies the first floor of what was once a showroom. At Sterling Place and Bedford Avenue, a handsome duo of buildings that now houses the New Life Tabernacle Church once housed automobile shops.

But the Studebaker Building across the street is the gem of Automobile Row. The landmarked building was built in a neo-Gothic style out of concrete and brick with a white terra cotta façade. Along the parapets at the top of the building you can still find the wheel logo of the Studebaker company. The front façade, which once had large windows to showcase cars, has been altered significantly and the building converted into apartments for low-income, disabled and homeless families.

CROWN FINISH CAVES
CHEESE TUNNELS

Aging cheese in old beer tunnels

925 Bergen Street #101
Brooklyn, NY 11238
www.crownfinishcaves.com
Transport: S to Park Place, A/C to Franklin Avenue

Just next door to the popular beer hall Berg'n, in an 1850s era tunnel under the former Nassau Brewery, cheese is aging thirty feet underground.

Opened in 2014, Crown Finish Caves is a licensed New York State dairy plant aging cheeses from places near and far. There are cheeses from the Hudson Valley, Vermont, Wisconsin, even Italy. The tunnels, which can be visited during special events, were originally excavated to age lager beer, but the brewery closed in 1914. The tunnel that Crown Finish Caves currently uses can hold 22,000 pounds of cheese, amidst a state-of-the-art renovation that keeps temperatures at about 50 degrees Fahrenheit and humidity at optimal levels.

The control system was built by Clauger, a family-owned French business that specializes in industrial refrigeration.

Crown Finish Caves ages the cheeses using the process of *affinage*, an old practice that involves much more than sitting in place. *The New York Times* describes the process of *affinage* as "a series of tedious, ritualized procedures (washing, flipping, brushing, patting, spritzing) that are meant to inch each wheel and wedge toward an apex of delectability."

The young cheeses, known as "green cheese" arrive at Crown Finish Caves when they are between one and fourteen days old. Aging can take over a year, but the time taken depends on the type of cheese. They mold the cheese into the shapes best known for each type of cheese.

In addition to the batch aging, Crown Finish Caves is helping producers experiment with new types of cheeses in small batches. They

also do testing within the *affinage* process, like bathing the cheeses in beer and cider, and washing them in salt brine.

Crown Finish Caves hopes to eventually use all five tunnels they have underground, increasing its capacity to around 100,000 pounds of cheese. Owners Benton Brown and Susan Boyle own the brewery building and for preservationists, it's exciting to see the adaptive reuse of this historical property, particularly amidst rapid real estate development in the area. The best way to be notified of upcoming events in the cheese tunnels is to subscribe to Crown Finish Caves' mailing list.

FRAGRANCE GARDEN
AT BROOKLYN BOTANIC

For best results, close your eyes

1000 Washington Avenue, Brooklyn
718-623-7200
www.bbg.org
Hours vary by season: see website

The Fragrance Garden in the Brooklyn Botanic was created for the nose, which generally doesn't get much special entertainment. It's an interesting question how many blind people take advantage of it, but without a doubt the provisions made for them—bronze identifying tags in Braille, and of course the choice and arrangement of plants—bring about in the rest of us a gentle mental shift. Here you can close your eyes and actually have a more intense experience.

The sense of smell has a noted power on the emotions, attributed to the proximity of the olfactory bulb to the brain's limbic system, where feelings and memories freely swirl. Many of the plants in the Fragrance Garden are compelling for suggesting smells that you already carry in your mind. Around the perimeter are large pots, each with several plants on a theme. One pot, tagged "Lemonade," has several citrusy species that evoke and are named after the lemon: lemon verbena, variegated lemon thyme, lemon bergamot. "Gently touch a leaf and smell the fragrance that rubs off onto your fingers," says the sign. "Does it smell good to you?" Yes. But when you sample one plant, lemon-scented geranium, your fingers smell not just like citrus, but—exactly, distinctly—lemonade. And not even natural lemonade: it's a dead ringer for the cheap, strong, artificial kind that comes in a foil packet and has a chemical aftertaste you could still detect from lunch while weed-whacking around the fence posts on a late summer afternoon when you were 13.

Where the garden might be content to keep pulling this evocative trick—you'll find plants that smell like root beer, pineapple, peppermint candy, almond, coconut, marshmallow—it goes further in explaining how the fragrances got there to begin with. When we toss rosemary in the sauce, the spice seems to have been created just for the certain zing it adds to our recipes. But when we exploit plants for special aromas and flavors, we're coming in at the end of a long, slow saga of secret chemical warfare. What teases our human brain might fry another. Even happy lemon is in on the game. "Some plant fragrances," says the sign, "act as self-defense. Lemon-scented plants have been known to keep away fleas, mosquitoes, ants and even cats." Knowing a thing like that makes the world a stranger place.

STATUE OF LIBERTY REPLICA AT BROOKLYN MUSEUM

A replica from 1900 in a parking lot

200 Eastern Parkway
Brooklyn, NY 11238
Wednesday–Sunday 11am–6pm, Thursday 11am–10pm
Transport: 2/3/4 to Eastern Parkway/Brooklyn Museum

In the middle of the parking lot of the Brooklyn Museum, accessed through Washington Avenue, is a replica of the Statue of Liberty that stands over 30 feet tall. It dates to 1900 – 14 years after the real Statue of Liberty was dedicated – and is part of the museum collection. For over one hundred years, the replica stood atop a building across from Lincoln Center. It was commissioned by a Russian-born auctioneer, William H. Flattau, for display atop a warehouse he ran at 43 West 64th Street, appropriately named Liberty Warehouse.

Unlike the original Statue of Liberty, designed in Paris by French sculptor Frederick Auguste Bartholdi (with help on the interior structure by engineer Gustav Eiffel), this version was cast in Salem, Ohio, by the firm W.H. Mullins. It is constructed of galvanized sheet steel over a steel frame, while the original has an iron skeleton covered in copper, 3/32 of an inch thick. Its dimensions are also a little different: the replica is slightly wider in the middle.

Kevin Stayton, Deputy Director at the Brooklyn Museum, says the difference between the two is partially because the replica was meant to be seen from below and because the casting process used in the Ohio version was less sophisticated than the techniques used to create the real Statue of Liberty.

To get the statue from Ohio to New York, it was cut in half, transported by truck then welded back together upon arrival. Like the famous statue, Flattau's version had a spiral staircase inside, which was open to the public until 1912. The torch was lit and guests could look outside through a small hole in the chin.

The eight-story warehouse was one of the tallest points in Manhattan when built and the replica Statue of Liberty ensured that it would become a landmark of sorts for the neighborhood. As the Brooklyn Museum describes, "Flattau thus combined his entrepreneurial spirit with pride in the adopted country in which he had prospered."

In 2002, real estate developers The Athena Group and Brickman Associates were looking to convert the warehouse into luxury rentals and co-op apartments.

The mini Statue of Liberty was donated to the Brooklyn Museum to honor the Fire Department of New York, New York Police Department, Emergency Medical Services, and the New York State Court Officers for their heroism on September 11, 2001.

With a new pedestal, Lady Liberty was installed in the Brooklyn Museum parking lot in 2005 as part of the Steinberg Family Sculpture Garden, where the remnants of Penn Station can also be found (see following double page).

REMNANT OF PENN STATION AT THE BROOKLYN MUSEUM

Artifacts of a lost train station

Brooklyn Museum
www.brooklynmuseum.org
Wednesday 11am-6pm, Thursday 11am-10pm, Friday Saturday and Sunday 11am-6pm
Transport: 2/3 subway to Eastern Parkway Brooklyn Museum

O n October 28th, 1963, demolition began on the original Pennsylvania Station, a glass, marble, granite and steel masterpiece by architectural firm McKim, Mead and White. The train station on the west side of Manhattan, only 53 years old, became a martyr for the landmarks preservation cause when the air rights to the station were sold after the Pennsylvania Railroad found itself in serious financial trouble. What was built instead was Madison Square Garden, with commuters constrained to an underground labyrinth. Architectural critic Vincent Scully famously described the contrast: "Through [the original station] one entered the city like a god ... One scuttles in now like rat."

Many enormous granite pieces from the station were simply dumped into the New Jersey Meadowlands and other places. Fortunately for posterity, the Brooklyn Museum has two remnants: the "Night" half of a "Day and Night" sculpture by Adolph A. Weinman, standing 11 feet tall, and a partial marble column from the waiting hall. The artifacts were recovered thanks to the efforts of the Anonymous Arts Recovery Society (AARS), a group of New York City creatives, led by influential New York gallery owner Ivan Karp. During the height of New York City's urban renewal, the Society was dedicated to salvaging the remnants of historical nineteenth-century architecture. The AARS, with federal tax-exempt status, obtained the Penn Station fragments by offering tax credits to Lipsett Incoporated, the contractor hired for the demolition of the station.

These remnants of Penn Station are placed among many other salvaged architectural sculptures including the Replica of the Statue of Liberty (see page 94) in the Steinberg Family Sculpture Garden, which you can access from the The Café in the Brooklyn Museum.

The remnants of Penn Station are scattered all over the United States. The 22 marble eagles were sent to new homes throughout the country. One façade clock was sent to an Eagle Scout Memorial in Kansas City, and half of one was found in a Bronx recycling depot in the 1990s. And more than a dozen original Penn Station remnants still exist inside the current station owing to the piecemeal demolition and construction – it was decreed that not a single day of train travel could be disrupted during the large infrastructural transformation. Amtrak only acknowledges a single remnant that remains, but insiders and transit enthusiasts know better. This all makes for a fun scavenger hunt you can take on a tour of the Remnants of Penn Station with Untapped Cities. Look for original staircases, handrails, fences, a stunning cast-iron partition, glass bricks, signage, marble eagles, and even an entire power plant hiding in plain sight. The Brooklyn Museum also has two decorative plaques from the exterior of Penn Station, also donated by Lipsett Incorporated, that are not on display.

THE BROOKLYN DAILY EAGLE

A piece of a newspaper history

Brooklyn Public Library
10 Grand Army Plaza
Brooklyn, NY 11238
Monday–Thursday 9am–9pm, Friday–Saturday 9am–6pm, Sunday 1pm–5pm
Transport: 2/3 Grand Army Plaza

An easily missed secret inside the Brooklyn Public Library at Grand Army Plaza is located just behind its two large bronze entrance doors; a giant eagle, with outspread wings, once stood above the doorway to the *Brooklyn Daily Eagle* headquarters.

The Brooklyn Public Library, which owes its existence partially to the newspaper, saved both the sculpture and the archives of the publication.

The *Brooklyn Daily Eagle* was once the city of Brooklyn's major newspaper. It was in publication from 1841 to 1955, beginning when Brooklyn was an independent city, through its incorporation into the City of New York, and past the Civil War, World War I and World War II. Writer Walt Whitman was one of the *Daily Eagle*'s early editors, serving from 1846 to 1848. He also contributed 800 pieces for the paper, including poems, editorials and news stories.

The *Daily Eagle's* first headquarters were on Old Fulton Street, near all of the major businesses of the era, close to the ferry (and later, the Brooklyn Bridge landing). In the newspaper's own words, in 1841, "Fulton Street was the single business thoroughfare. Court Street was unknown. Sands Street was the residence of the aristocrats; the Heights were a bluff merely; Fulton Street, beyond City Hall, was a country road, and Myrtle Avenue an adventurous highway of travel to Fort Greene."

By the Civil War, the *Brooklyn Daily Eagle* was the largest evening newspaper in America. By the 1890s, Brooklyn was the third largest city in the country.

With the rise of the new skyscrapers in Downtown Brooklyn, the *Brooklyn Daily Eagle* moved its headquarters to a new eight-story building at the corner of Washington Street and Johnson Street. The Landmarks Preservation Commission states that although the second headquarters of the *Daily Eagle* were demolished, it was one of the buildings that "helped popularize the Beaux-Arts classicism" of later skyscrapers here.

Across from Grimaldi's and Juliana's pizzerias, you'll still find the Eagle Warehouse & Storage Company building, a brick fire-proof warehouse that was built around the old *Daily Eagle* pressroom. It was converted into a condominium building in in 1980.

The *Brooklyn Daily Eagle* supported numerous major civic movements in the 19th century, including the construction of the Brooklyn Bridge and most importantly, for this story, the creation of a central library at Grand Army Plaza. This library broke ground in 1911 but would not be completed until 1941. The two large bronze entrance doors are the library's most recognizable feature, adorned with symbols representing some of the most famous characters in literary history.

The *Brooklyn Daily Eagle* that is in publication today is unaffiliated with the original, having purchased the name when it entered the public domain.

EBBETS FIELD FLAGPOLE

A Dodgers relic, relocated

Intersection of Atlantic Avenue and Flatbush Avenue
Transport: 2/3/4/5 to Atlantic Avenue - Barclays Center

In the 1950s, Brooklyn Dodgers owner Walter O'Malley hoped to build a new stadium for his team at Atlantic Yards but was rebuffed by Robert Moses, who was strong-arming him to move the team to Flushing. The Dodgers hightailed it to Los Angeles, where they remain today, but in an ironic twist of fate, the Ebbets Field flagpole now stands on O'Malley's intended site.

When Ebbets Field was demolished in 1960 (see page 84), this center-field flagpole was donated to a Veteran of Foreign Wars (VFW) outpost on Utica Avenue in East Flatbush. There it sat for almost 50 years, occasionally sought out on personal pilgrimages by Brooklyn Dodgers enthusiasts. Even after the VFW outpost closed, the flagpole stayed put. The outpost was repurposed into a casket making company and later a church.

One of the few that knew of the flagpole's existence was Brooklyn Borough President Marty Markowitz, a Crown Heights native and former New York State senator. As plans to redevelop Atlantic Yards (now known as Pacific Park) were underway, Markowitz knew that the flagpole would be a fitting piece of memorabilia at the new Barclays Center stadium. He also knew that the VFW building was going to be demolished.

In 2007, Pacific Park developer Bruce Ratner bought the flagpole and had a new base installed. In 2012, the flagpole was unveiled in a ceremony attended by Jackie Robinson's daughter, Sharon Robinson, along with Brooklyn Nets player Jerry Stackhouse (who wears Robinson's #42), Ratner, Markowitz and others. The plaque, which serves as a little pat on the back, reads: "This flagpole stood in Ebbets Field until Brooklyn's famed ballpark was torn down in 1960. Bruce C. Ratner and Borough President Marty Markowitz are proud to permanently place this historic symbol of the Brooklyn Dodgers at the borough's new home for major professional sports."

The move not only locates the flagpole closer than ever to the original Ebbets Field, it is also where it may have moved to had the Dodgers stayed in Brooklyn.

INDIAN FACES
ON THE MONTAUK CLUB

A tribute to an Indian tribe

25 Eighth Avenue
Brooklyn, NY 11217
www.montaukclub.com
Check website for membership details. Free for clergy; reduced for those
with residences outside New York City. Regular events hosted by outside
organizations.
Transport: 2/3 subway to Grand Army Plaza

On the corner of Eighth Avenue and Lincoln Place in Park Slope, just off Grand Army Plaza, is the Montauk Club, a Venetian Gothic palazzo-inspired private club built in 1891. Included among the notable people who have stepped through these doors are United States Presidents John F. Kennedy, Dwight D. Eisenhower, Grover Cleveland, and William McKinley, all of whom gave speeches.

The club has regular events for members as well as events hosted by outside organizations, which is your best way to visit. If you do get a chance to go inside, one of the nicest places in the club is the second floor balcony off the main dining room, where you can enjoy a drink while looking out across the green canopy of Prospect Park.

The Montauk Club was founded in 1888 in the tradition of private clubs at the height of the Gilded Age. The club is named after the Montauk Indians from Long Island.

The exterior design of the club was inspired by the Ca d'Oro – also known as the Palazzo Santa Sofia – on the Grand Canal in Venice. The architectural influence can be most clearly seen in the quatrefoil shape of the windows and pointed arches on the façade. But look closely and you will see references to the Montauk Indians on much of the building's exterior: terra cotta faces peer out from atop columns and above the main entrance, while a wraparound frieze between the third and fourth floors features scenes related to the Indian tribe. The cast iron fence that wraps around the building also shows Indian faces. In 2004 Chief Robert Pharoah, representing the tribe, was a guest at the 115th anniversary celebration of the club.

The Montauk Club was designed by Frances H. Kimball, a notable architect whose famous buildings still stand in New York City today, including the Trinity and U.S. Realty Buildings on Broadway and the Corbin Building next to Fulton Center.

Today, the Montauk Club is now part condominium and part private club, with residents entering through what was originally the ladies' entrance, just to the left of the main doors.

The interiors of the Montauk Club are often seen in film and on television in shows such as Boardwalk Empire and The Knick.

FORAGING WITH WILDMAN STEVE BRILL

Unique food tour

Prospect Park
www.wildmanstevebrill.com

"**W**ildman" Steve Brill has been giving foraging tours in New York City's parks since 1982, with an aim to educate the public about urban agriculture, renewable resources, and sustainable eating. Long before the farm-to-table movement, Brill began the tours with the approval of New York City Parks Commissioner Gordon Davis, the first African American to serve in that role.

But Davis' successor, Henry Stern, wanted to shut Brill down, sending undercover rangers to catch him in the act. Brill was arrested on a tour in 1986 for picking dandelions, carrots, daylily shoots, cranberries and other wild produce.

Brill and Stern came to a detente of sorts: Brill would join the Parks Department staff as its naturalist and continue to give tours, sticking to "plentiful species." Four years and another Parks Commissioner later, Brill quit and went freelance. These days, although foraging is illegal in New York City's parks, the tours happen through a tacit acceptance between Brill and the park rangers.

Guests on Brill's tours range from residents and tourists, to school classes and university groups. In Prospect Park you can find "Lamb's quarters," which can be used for flavoring soups and salads, shepherd's purse, wood sorrel, and poor man's pepper, a mustard that is also said to have cancer-fighting properties. Brill shares relevant recipes while on the foraging tour – elderberries found can be used in pancakes and sassafras for homemade root beer. Guests bring their own bags and containers and take home their finds.

Most importantly, Brill shows guests how to identify plants that are dangerous to humans, not just the poisonous ones but also those that can cause indigestion and illness. Because edible and poisonous plants look similar, it's important to start your foraging education with an expert.

Brill is not only experienced in botany; his drawings and models have been shown in art exhibits, museums and botanical gardens. He has written four books on food foraging, including a cookbook. Brill is also a jazz musician and on tours he just might perform the Brillophone, an instrument made by cupping the hands. In a past life, Brill was a tournament chess player. With all these eclectic experiences, it's not surprising that Brill's tours are both entertaining (he has a penchant for puns) and adventurous.

Brill gives tours not only of Prospect Park, but also of other parks in and outside New York City. You can also download the Wild Edibles Forage app, made by Brill, for your own adventuring.

REMNANTS OF THE PARK SLOPE PLANE CRASH

A jet age disaster

Sterling Place between 6th and 7th Avenues
Transport: 2/3 to Grand Army Plaza, B/Q to 7th Avenue

In the heart of Park Slope, the scars of a 1960 plane crash have been all but repaired, erased or built over. But some remnants are still visible. The largest is in the brickwork atop 126 Sterling Place, where the right wing of the plane tore through. The repair was done in a different color and material to its adjacent twin building, and its black cornice is completely missing.

Brick columns at 123 Sterling Place (built in 1920) also show evidence of patching up, but the most unique remnants are in the backyard of sculptor Steve Keltner, who lives on the street. One particular remnant salvaged from the churchyard he calls the *"pièce de résistance"*. Lying against a fence is part of the plane's right wing. A label next to the gasket is still legible: "No. 5 main tank Auxiliary Fuel. Structural limit 17,605 lbs."

In addition to another large piece in the back yard, Keltner keeps a smaller one inside his apartment that he believes was part of a chair inside the plane. The grates on the front window of his apartment are also notable: they come from the original wrought iron gate of the Pillar of Fire Church, which Steve removed and installed at his place, making the circular modifications.

As the age of jet travel was ramping up in 1960, a deadly mid-flight plane crash over New York would temporarily dampen the fervor. It was December 16, 1960, one day before the 57th anniversary of the

Wright Brothers' first flight. A United Airlines DC-8 and a TWA Super Constellation collided, likely over Staten Island. The DC-8 was coming from Chicago O'Hare bound for Idlewild Airport, now John F. Kennedy Airport. The Super Constellation was going from Columbus, Ohio to LaGuardia Airport.

The TWA plane crashed at Miller Field on the southern coast of Staten Island with no survivors. The DC-8 made it all the way to Park Slope, where it came down on Sterling Place near the intersection of 7th Avenue. Devastation to this dense residential area was significant. Ten brownstones went aflame, along with a funeral home, a deli, and a laundromat. The prophetically-named Pillar of Fire Church located mid-block was completely destroyed. A 90-year-old caretaker of the church was killed, one of six casualties on the ground.

There was one initial survivor from the crash in Brooklyn; Stephen Lambert Baltz, an 11-year-old boy from Illinois, who was thrown out of the plane onto a snow bank. He succumbed to pneumonia the next day.

One hundred and thirty-four people lost their lives, making it the deadliest air accident to date at the time. It would also be the first to be investigated using the "black box" flight recorder. It is known that the DC-8 had been requested to fly into a holding pattern and appeared to have missed the mark, possibly due to equipment failure either on the plane or on the ground.

Although no plaque exists on Sterling Place, commemorative markers have been placed elsewhere in Brooklyn: United Airlines purchased a lot in Green-Wood Cemetery to bury the unidentified remains; in 2010, the cemetery erected a memorial to the victims of the plane crash; and in the chapel of New York Methodist Hospital, where Stephen Baltz died, there is a plaque embedded with four dimes and five nickels, which the boy had in his pocket when the plane crashed.

The New York Times.

127 DIE AS 2 AIRLINERS COLLIDE OVER CITY; JET SETS BROOKLYN FIRE, KILLING 5 OTHERS; SECOND PLANE CRASHES ON STATEN ISLAND

STEPHEN BALTZ MEMORIAL

The boy who survived

New York Methodist Hospital, Brooklyn
718-780-3000
www.nym.org
Transport: G train/7th Av

On December 16, 1960, two commercial airplanes – a TWA Constellation, and a newly issued United Airlines DC-8 jet (see page, 106-107) – collided in the air over Staten Island. The first plane crashed immediately; the jet continued to lose altitude over Brooklyn until it began clipping the tops of buildings, finally hurtling through an intersection in Park Slope, spreading fire, debris, and bodies.

The newspaper photos of the disaster are surreal. Astonished onlookers stand among fire hoses and the rubble of toppled brownstones, the jet's enormous tail fin jutting out of the smoking street. One photo shows a young boy sitting in a daze, an older couple leaning over to shelter him with an umbrella. This was 11-year-old Stephen Baltz, later to be known as "the boy who survived." Incredibly, Baltz, who was traveling alone to New York to meet his family, was thrown from the jet and landed in a snow bank. All of the other passengers and the crews of both planes died, as well as six people on the ground: 134 in all. It was the worst air disaster in United States history, and the first involving a passenger jet.

"We are grateful to the Almighty for this miraculous thing that has happened to our son," Mr. Baltz said after Stephen was taken to nearby Methodist Hospital to treat his burns and broken leg. During the night the boy was lucid, even describing to caregivers that rarest experience: what it's like to be in a falling jetliner. "I remember looking out the plane window at the snow below covering the city," he said. "It looked like a picture out of a fairy book. Then all of a sudden there was an explosion ... I held on to my seat and then the plane crashed." Stephen Baltz died at 10am the next morning, probably due to fuel burns on his lungs.

Before he left, Baltz's father dropped the contents of the boy's pocket in the chapel's poor box. Four dimes and five nickels: 65 cents. The chaplain mounted the coins on a bronze plaque which can be seen on the wall today: the smallest, most personal monument in New York City.

PARK SLOPE VETERANS MUSEUM ⑯

Hidden museum in the Park Slope armory

361 15th Street
Brooklyn, NY 11215
www.parkslopeveteransmuseum.net
By appointment only (contact via website)
Transport: F/G to 15th Street-Prospect Park

To visit the Park Slope Armory is to walk amid history and to witness the building's rebirth. Wood and glass cases that once held rifles now display children's artwork from the YMCA. Possibly one of the least known places in Brooklyn is here too: the Park Slope Veterans Museum, which is open by appointment only.

Tom Miskel, a Park Slope resident and veteran of the Vietnam War, has been actively expanding, archiving and organizing the multi-room museum since he arrived, also serving as a de-facto historian for the armory. The place is chock full of artifacts from the many wars fought by the United States, though, as Miskel recounts, there was a period of time when artifacts were finding their way out of the armory and getting sold – but he has managed to recover many of the items from a shop in Virginia. Other items have been donated by veterans or by their families.

The main room of the collection has an incredible number of items on display. A back room is dedicated to the Civil War, with models in uniform wearing the red pants from which the 14th Regiment gets its nickname. There are swords, toy soldiers, and other memorabilia organized and neatly displayed.

The front room is divided into sections by conflict, with notable photographs, documents, helmets, and life-size models in uniform. There is a particularly sobering collection of Nazi paraphernalia brought back by soldiers from World War II.

The main hallway of the museum is situated just next to the women's shelter, separated from it by a wooden railing that once stood in the abandoned shooting gallery. This hallway contains more military models, flags and memorials both inside and outside the display cases that form part of the overall collection.

Miskel has a particular interest in the lesser-known stories from the wars, such as the service of black soldiers in World War I and that of female pilots in World War II. Today, Miskel is working on improving the library and hopes to make it a destination for military research. He's also expanding the display on the Korean War. He hopes to have more informational videos made and more screens installed to tell the history of the 14th Regiment and the armory overall.

The Park Slope Armory was home to the 14th Regiment of the New York State militia, a volunteer regiment that fought in American conflicts from the Civil War to World War I. Their nickname, the "Red Legged Devils," was bestowed upon them by Stonewall Jackson, the famous Confederate general, for their persistence at the First Battle of Bull Run.

17

PARK SLOPE ARMORY'S ABANDONED SHOOTING GALLERY

An incredible place

361 15th Street
Brooklyn, NY 11215
In the Veterans Museum, ask the head of it to take you down there. He'll some-times accept.
Transport: F/G to 15th Street-Prospect Park

O ne of the city's many armories, the Park Slope Armory encompasses an entire city block in Brooklyn, bounded by 7th and 8th Avenues, and 14th and 15th Streets. Originally built for the 14th Regiment of the New York State militia in 1893, it now houses sports facilities run by the YMCA, along with a women's shelter. But one of the building's most impressive secrets lies on the lower level of the armory. Left fallow for many years, a long shooting gallery allowed for short-range and long-range target practice. Its entrance sits behind a locked door, through a hallway long repurposed as a storage space, and down a decorative wooden staircase. It's an incredible place, silent from years of abandonment but aching for future use.

There is a dusty Victorian-style waiting room that has retained its tin walls and ceilings, green tinted paint job, and wooden wraparound bench. There was also once a wooden railing here that has since been moved to the first floor of the armory, next to the Veterans Museum, an equally unknown spot (see page 106). The words "EASTERN DISTRICT" printed on the left refer to the militia's district within New York State.

Under a large pipe, possibly over a century old, you enter an arched brick hallway that runs alongside both shooting galleries. On the right, there are some unused spaces with crumbling wooden walls. The short range shooting gallery is located to the left. Small staircases once led to a sort of half floor, now somewhat collapsed, from which the targets would be raised into the shooting galleries themselves. Further along, the ceilings of the hallway get lower and lower until you actually have to duck through an opening to proceed.

Along this section, electrical lighting appears for the first time, hanging alongside the overhead pipes. On the right, there is a heavy metal door that leads into a small room, possibly used once as a holding cell, according to the armory historian, though this is unconfirmed. Scenes from the 1990 movie *Goodfellas*, where the character Paulie is in prison, were filmed in this abandoned area.

The long-range shooting gallery, located just to the left of this hallway, is barely lit. Standing in the dark, barrel-vaulted space, you can almost hear the voices and shots of men practicing their trade. Bullet holes still remain in large metal pieces that line parts of the ceiling and the end of the gallery.

18

THE WOODEN HOUSES
OF WEBSTER PLACE

A touch of San Francisco

21-31 Webster Place
Brooklyn, NY 11215
Transport: R to Prospect Avenue, F/G to 15th Street-Prospect Park

In a rare disruption to the street grid in Park Slope, the area bounded by 16th Street, Prospect Avenue, 6th Avenue and 7th Avenue has two mid-block streets: Webster Place and Jackson Place. These streets were not extant in an 1855 or an 1866 map of Brooklyn, although notes on an 1880 map indicate that plans for the two streets were filed in 1853. However, the two streets do appear in an 1869 map, along with the placement of some of the first homes. In 1872, a motion was made for the "opening" (likely meaning a widening) of both of these streets to Prospect Avenue.

The layout of Webster Place, and its location just about a block from Prospect Expressway, makes the discovery of this quaint street all the more surprising. Equally surprising is the presence of a stretch of six beautiful Queen Anne-style wooden houses, each with a front porch and colorful detailing. Some even have working wooden shutters. These homes date to the late 1860s.

The street was was originally cobblestone, as a writer to the *Brooklyn Daily Eagle* reminisces in 1943: "What a wonderful old place that little street was and how nice and neat it was. The cobblestones were swept clean every morning." In response, another reader concurred and added that there were "shade trees on both sides and one-family, two-story houses halfway from 16th Street, and the other half, two-story and basement houses to Prospect Avenue." A grocer on the corner of 16th Street and Webster Place would deliver goods by sleigh in the snow.

Vintage photographs from 1929 show that there used to be two sets of the wooden houses, lining both sides of the streets. Though the trees on the street still form "an arch over the roadway," as they did in the recollection of another resident in 1943, the original wooden houses on the eastern side of the street are gone.

This area is not part of the landmarked Park Slope Historic, but the remaining six homes have been painstakingly renovated by their owners over the years.

BARACK OBAMA'S FORMER TOWNHOUSE

"When I was living here, Brooklyn was cool, but not this cool."

640 2nd Street
Brooklyn, NY 11215
Transport: 2/3 to Grand Army Plaza

In the mid-1980s, after graduating Columbia University, Barack Obama moved to a brownstone in Park Slope with his then-girlfriend Genevieve Cook, an Australian he met at a Christmas party in the East Village in 1983. She was a teacher of second and third graders at the Brooklyn Friends School. Obama would start a new job at the New York Public Interest Group, a non-profit where he would begin to flex his community organizing muscles.

As recounted in the book *Barack Obama: The Story* by David Maraniss, Cook rented the apartment on the top floor of 640 2nd Street, just steps from Prospect Park, in the spring of 1984. The townhouse, owned by a colleague of Cook's, was built sometime around 1901 to 1903 and is a classic three-story brownstone with bowed windows.

In December 1984, Barack quit his first post-college job at the Business International Corporation and moved into the Park Slope townhouse, in what was meant to be a temporary arrangement. However, he stayed until March 1985, when Genevieve moved to another apartment on Warren Street in Brooklyn. He helped her move but got his own place in Hell's Kitchen, Manhattan and they broke up by May of 1985. Maraniss explains, "Their time living together did not go well." Entries published from Cook's diary show Obama searching for his identity and purpose in this world. Cook found him "withholding" on the emotional front. But within a few months, Obama would relocate to Chicago, taking a job with the Developing Communities Project, starting on the path that would take him all the way to the White House.

Today, as it did in the 1980s during Obama's tenure, the brownstone at 640 blends in with the rest of 2nd Street. As reported in the *New York Times* in 2012, when the apartment was revealed in Maraniss' book, the current tenants as well as neighbors were hearing of Obama's occupancy for the first time. On a visit to Brooklyn as President of the United States, Obama told students at the Pathways in Technology Early College High School, "When I was living here, Brooklyn was cool, but not this cool."

THE MYSTERY OF THE GRAFFITI TOWNHOUSE

Vacant but beautified

472 2nd Street
Brooklyn, NY 11215
Transport: D/N/R to Union Street

In Park Slope, it's rare to find an unoccupied townhouse, so in demand is Brooklyn real estate. The home at 472 2nd Street not only falls into this category, it's also almost completely plastered in vibrant street art. The property has sat seemingly unoccupied for as long as people appear to remember. Repeated complaints to the Department of Buildings in the first decade of the 2000s (viewable online to the public) indicate a lack of maintenance for the building cited as "vacant," and "abandoned." Nonetheless, real estate website StreetEasy lists a rental from 2010 with interior photos of a top floor unit in great condition.

What is known from public records is that the townhouse between 6th and 7th Avenues is owned by a former art teacher and long time resident of Park Slope. From the 1970s to 1990s, she ran a dive bar known as the Landmark Pub in a nearby building, which, after years of abandonment, was sold to a developer for $4.2 million. It's possible that the family is holding out for a similar flip here at 472.

Regardless, there is clearly a semblance of creativity and whimsy to this circa 1920 townhouse, a fun respite from the perfectly beautified townhouses along this street. Given that the building is owned by an artist, we like to think it's her handiwork.

The mural here showed up sometime after 2011. There are bursts of colorful flowers, bird designs and abstract patterns. They surround somewhat foreboding metal cages and grills (spray painted of course) attached to the windows on the first two floors, onto which are warning signs alleging recording of all activity. Even the fence surrounding the lot is sprayed and small sculptures adorn the building façade.

At one point, a rental sign appeared, unaffiliated with any real estate brokerage, offering space for commercial, office or medical.

A similarly painted townhouse is at 46 4th Street, a gallery previously run by the daughter of the owner.

SECRET WRITING LAB INSIDE THE BROOKLYN SUPERHERO SUPPLY CO.

A secret identity for 826NYC

372 5th Avenue
Brooklyn, NY 11215
www.superherosupplies.com
Transport: D/N/R to 9th Street, F/G to 4th Avenue

f you're 8, 18, or 80, and decide the next big step in your life trajectory is to become a superhero, the perfect one-stop shop to ensure success can be found tucked away in Park Slope on 5th Avenue between 5th and 6th Streets. Brooklyn's Superhero Supply Co., an unassuming free-standing store, is often mistaken for a hardware store. It actually houses shelves of fun things: cans of Courage, Gumption, invisibility paint, and tools to help you scale walls. A mock seriousness to the store, paired with the Willy Wonka-like fantasy world, creates a delightful place to explore and play.

The store is actually a secret identity of 826NYC, a not-for-profit writing lab that focuses on kids aged 6 to 18. Accessed via a trick bookshelf, the lab offers free after school drop-in one-on-one tutoring and fun weeknight and weekend workshops that encourage creativity and writing of all kinds: short stories, films, comics, and even Japanese Manga. 826 will also host class field trips that aid teachers in planning creative writing exercises. The organization is active in several cities through the United States; the original location, 826 Valencia in San Francisco, is fronted by a pirate store.

Beyond the basics, you definitely want to check this place out. If you're into design, the whole store is filled with examples of coherent and beautiful graphic design. Products and signs have a tongue-in-cheek playfulness that will definitely bring a smirk or a smile to your face. Don't know where to begin? Pick up the Superhero Starter Kit, which comes with a ready-made secret identity, cape, mask and blaster. But you'll soon want to upgrade, maybe with some Super X-Ray Glasses or a can of Time Travel. The "brands" carried by the Superhero Store have fabulous names too, such as Bugayenko Laboratories and FantastiCo!, each appropriately named for the products they supposedly produce.

If you love the written word, 826 has shelves of essay and short story collections written by its students and other great modern writers linked to 826's founder, writer Dave Eggers. If you don't need any superhero supplies, you can play with several of the store's interactive exhibits: try on a cape and snap a pic for your friends at the cape testing chamber. And if you're feeling villainous, the store has a cure! A de-villainizing chamber asks you a series of questions to determine the nature of your villainy then takes cares of the problem. Even purchasing something small is an experience, as store rules require you to recite the vow of heroism with every purchase.

CARROLL STREET BRIDGE

The oldest of the three retractable bridges left in the United States

Brooklyn, NY 11231
Transport: R subway to Union Street

"**A**ny Person Driving over this Bridge Faster than a Walk will be Subject to a Penalty of Five Dollars For Each Offence" reads the central sign on the Carroll Street Bridge in Gowanus. The sign refers to an antiquated law that dates back to the early 1800s. The bridge itself dates to 1889.

The wood plank deck bridge is the only wooden bridge in all of New York City that allows cars to cross, and is the oldest of the three retractable bridges left in the United States.

With such credentials it was designated a New York City landmark in 1987. Belgian block lines the roads leading up to the bridge, and amidst the raw, industrial state of the Gowanus Canal, you can easily imagine the bridge in use during the 19th and early 20th centuries.

Retractable, or retractile bridges open to allow water vessels to pass through; the Carroll Street Bridge uses a mechanism that rolls the whole span of the bridge diagonally on wheels along steel rails using pulleys and wire cables. It was originally powered by steam, but was converted to electric in 1907-08. Inferring from historic documents, a retractable bridge was likely constructed here because an earlier design for the bridge would have required the acquisition of a piece of private property that the Common Council was having trouble purchasing at the time.

The Landmarks Preservation Commission noted that retractable bridges are "employed to provide channel clearance in locations where other bridge types are impractical."

The Carroll Street Bridge is an example of a trapezoidal-shaped retractable bridge. It spans 107 feet with a steel overhead stay frame in a latticework pattern that supports steel cables. There are two pedestrian walkways, also of wood, and the steel is painted in a bright blue.

Many notable names were involved in the construction of the Carroll Street Bridge. Robert van Buren (a descendant of United States President Martin van Buren), Chief Engineer of the Bureau of Construction, oversaw the project. Notable civil engineer Charles O.H. Fritzche developed the mechanical system. A subsidiary of Cooper, Hewitt & Company, New Jersey Steel and Iron, manufactured the steel.

In the 1980s the bridge was in such poor shape it had to be closed to traffic, but a renovation took place just in time for its 100th anniversary.

Have the bridge open for you

Today, the bridge is operated by the New York City Department of Transportation (NYC DOT). When someone needs a bridge opened in order to pass, they must contact the DOT two hours in advance.

The Carroll Street Bridge is one of five bridges on the Gowanus Canal that are movable (the others either lift or split apart). In addition to walking across the bridge, one of the best ways to experience it is by kayaking with the Gowanus Dredgers (see page 130). From below, you can see the infrastructure of the historic bridge up close and personal.

REMAINING WALL
OF THE BROOKLYN TIP-TOPS

23

Remnant of a Brooklyn baseball field

Third Avenue between 1st and 3rd Street
Brooklyn, NY 11215
Transport: D/N/R to 9th Street, F/G to 4 Avenue

Until 2009, it was believed that a brick wall on Third Avenue between 1st and 3rd Street in Gowanus was a remnant of the stadium at Washington Park, where the Brooklyn Dodgers played from 1898 to 1912 before the team moved to Ebbets Field. Though still historical, the wall is now believed to have been built at Washington Park for the players of the Brooklyn Tip-Tops, a Federal League team that played from 1914 to 1915.

The historical wall is made of two distinct sections. One has a series of arched windows, now bricked up. The other, closer to First Street, has evenly spaced engaged columns with square parapets that emerge above the wall.

The Tip-Tops were owned by Robert Ward, the proprietor of the New York City-based Ward Baking Company that sold certain products under the label Tip-Top. The short-lived Federal League folded in 1915 after just three years, suffering from financial problems while embroiled in an antitrust lawsuit against the American and National leagues.

Photos from the Tip-Tops era indicate that the windowed wall was the backside of the bleachers, with the openings possibly for horses, and that both parts of the wall likely date to 1914, after the Dodgers left. Ensconced within the parapet portion of the wall was the scoreboard for the game, with advertisements painted on the inside of the wall.

Some believe that the wall was part of a carriage house or clubhouse that may have been standing in the Dodgers era, but a detailed analysis of vintage photographs and maps done by Andrew Ross and David Dyte of *Brooklyn Ballparks* seems to shows otherwise. They write, "We hate to say this, because we wish it weren't so, but in our considered view that's not a Dodger wall." Author Brian Merlis, who focuses in Brooklyn history agrees, telling the *Daily News*, "I can say with absolute certainty that this wall was not part of Washington Park prior to [Dodgers'] departure."

Con Edison purchased the land that contained Washington Park in 1922 and continues to operate a parking lot there. In spite of the demolition of some buildings in the property in 2009, Con Edison pledged to keep the wall standing. The wall, of which about half remains, is now the backside to a loading dock. Painted in a pale pink, the wall is an easily missed piece of history in the rapidly developing, post-industrial neighborhood.

THE COIGNET BUILDING

24

The oldest known concrete building in New York City

360 Third Avenue
Brooklyn, NY 11215
Transport: D/N/R to 9th Street or Union Street

Before the Whole Foods in Gowanus was built, a handsome building stood alone, left over from the bustling concrete industry that came before. But more than just another pretty Neoclassical building, the Coignet Building was actually a showcase for a new material that took the building industry by storm in the 19th century. It is the oldest known concrete building in New York City.

Moulded concrete, or *beton-coignet* as it was called in France, was patented by French industrialist François Coignet, the first in the world to use iron-reinforced concrete as a technique in construction. It consisted of a mix of sand, lime and cement. Beton concrete was showcased to much acclaim at the 1867 Exposition Universelle de Paris.

Though many people were experimenting with similar mixes, Coignet made it possible to mass produce large pieces of concrete and pioneered the use of iron reinforcements. Coignet's particular mix, perfected through many tests, was found to be particularly durable, adaptable and affordable. The material could be molded instead of painstakingly shaped with chisels and cutting tools. A cement wash could also be applied to color the concrete, giving it the appearance of granite, brownstone or whatever was desired.

Completed in 1873, the Coignet Building was once part of a five-acre factory along the Gowanus Canal operated by the New York and Long Island Coignet Stone Company. The building functioned as both an office and a prototype. The detailing on the exterior referenced numerous architectural styles popular at the time, in order to show the possibilities of the material.

On the two façades that face the street, there are two Ionic-columned porticos topped by a pediment. Quoining along the edges of the building give it a Neo-Renaissance influence. The staircase leads up to rounded doors, a shape that is mirrored on the first floor windows.

On the second floor, both the rounded and rectangular windows are framed by columns and Italianate window-heads. The whole building is topped by a relatively simple entablature. It is believed that the original floors were possibly made of concrete as well.

For many years, the Coignet Building was covered in a faux-brick, which concealed the concrete façade. The building was renovated by Whole Foods as part of a deal to purchase the land. Its completion was long awaited by local residents.

Work by the Coignet Stone Company can still be found today in some of the city's most famous landmarks – the American Museum of Natural History, the Metropolitan Museum of Art, the Cleft Ridge Span in Prospect Park and Saint Patrick's Cathedral.

THE INTERFERENCE ARCHIVE

A place dedicated to social movements

131 8th Street #4
Brooklyn, NY 11215
Thursday 1pm–9pm, Friday–Sunday 12pm–5pm
Transport: F/G/R to Smith-9th Street

Tucked inside a building that the Department of Buildings officially lists as having zero floors, the Interference Archive aims to

capture the relationship between social movements and cultural production. The collection contains materials from social movements all
around the world, extending far beyond the usual suspects like anar-
chism or peace movements. Here you can also find information about
more obscure topics like punk feminism and bike advocacy. And it's
not all lefty material – there is a section on the Tea Party and white
supremacy – not that the founders support those ideologies.

There are the usual things one would expect in an archive – stacks
of books and ephemera used in social movements (buttons, posters,
T-shirts, bumper stickers, photographs, even board games). But there
is also something decidedly old-school and laid back about this archive.

That's because the archive began as a personal collection by a Brooklyn couple, Josh MacFee and his girlfriend Dara Greenwald, who passed
away in 2011. The current location was an outgrowth of their apartment, which was so renown that PhD students would research from it.

The items are all accessible in open stacks and drawers rather than
preserved in glass cases. Today, there are over 45,000 items – with
only a portion digitized. Some of the highlights include a collection
of vintage posters collected by Carlos Vega and a holographic Hillary
Clinton button.

There have been over 16 exhibitions in the two-room space, along
with regular events and workshops. The Interference Archive lives on,
funded by members who make small monthly donations, and staffed
by volunteers. No appointment is necessary, just drop by.

A hidden alley along the Gowanus canal not labeled on any map

There are only a few places to cross the Gowanus Canal, New
York City's most famous environmental cleanup site. One of
those crossings is the 9th Street bridge, below the Smith-9th
Street viaduct, home to the highest subway station in the City.
Just before the crossing, there's an opening in the industrial wall
beneath a large roll-down metal door. Signs point to firms like
Serett Metalworks and BigReuse, but for the average passerby it
doesn't seem like a place to visit. That's how Gowanus is: places
that look private may actually be public. Roads labeled on official
city maps are reused for parking and other purposes.

Alongside one of the basins of the Gowanus Canal is a de-facto alley,
formed by the vacant space between warehouses. It's an unmapped
"street" within an industrial and manufacturing property that leads
out to a parking lot. Planters, benches and ivy growing on the walls
of the warehouses make this alley a welcoming contrast to the
industrial buildings that surround it.

The periodic table of chemicals

2nd Street and canal, Brooklyn
718-243-0849; call ahead for canoeing schedule
www.gowanuscanal.org
Admission and canoe rental: free
Transport: F and G trains/Carroll St

The Gowanus Canal is so polluted, and has been for so long, its foulness has garnered a whole body of local legend. Some say the waterway is a dump for the mafia's guns and corpses; there's a tale of a city diver emerging with his skin melted off; one recent investigator (wearing, notably, a "dry suit" so none of the water could touch him) was alarmed to find that the channel had no discernible bottom, just very deep, very black ooze. A local nonprofit group, the Gowanus Dredgers, is undaunted: they offer free canoeing and kayaking from a convenient waterfront on 2nd Street.

"The spirit I have is that I like to canoe," says Owen Foote, the group's treasurer and one of the founding members. "This waterway looked fun and safe and close, so why not take advantage of it?" The safety of the water can be disputed, but the ecological miscarriage is, strange to say, part of the appeal. When you canoe the Gowanus, you're on the scene of a vast crime against nature. It's a little dangerous, like trespassing. The canal became an industrial sewer in the late 1800s, and remains to this day a site of heavy dumping when rains flush untreated sewage into the river system. Asked what kinds of pollutants float here, Foote says, "Basically anything you flush down the toilet. On the bottom it's a periodic table of chemicals." If this sounds terrible, it's also interesting, and the Dredgers are wise to the appeal. Already instrumental in reactivating the canal's circulating water pump, they know that the more people come for recreation, the easier it will be to fund a proper clean-up. "It's all about attention and awareness," says Foote. "What better way to get people aware and involved than through canoeing and kayaking?"

To begin, you have to sign a waiver – usually a sign you are about to do something fun. As you watch the gritty bridges and Brooklyn skyline glide past, you will paddle ugly water. Near the bay are colorful blooms of oil; the inland channel is soupy and toiletsome, and smells like whatever a century of hell-bent industry smells like. But when it strikes you that you are seeing the city as few ever will, and you spot the geese, egrets, and crabs that have rebounded here since the Dredgers arrived, you'll get it.

The Gowanus Canal is named for Gowane, the sachem of the Canarsie tribe of Lenape Indians who fished and farmed here.

27

THE HOBBIT DOORS
OF DENNET PLACE

A tiny lane with curiously small doors

Located just behind the Gowanus Canal

Near the industrial edge of the Gowanus Canal, in an area bounded by the sky-high Gowanus Expressway and an elevated subway line, is a tiny lane. Until recent years, the entire street was like an ethnic micro-enclave, inhabited by a tight-knit community of Italian Americans. The most obvious curiosity is the existence of tiny doors about four feet tall, affectionately referred to as "hobbit doors," beneath the concrete staircases that lead to the main floors of the houses.

Each door is slightly different and they don't just vary by color. Some doors have brass knockers, others just a street number. Some have a mail slot, while others have small window or two. The majority of them have an accompanying tiny window, varying in size and shape.

Neighborhood change has altered the demographic of Dennet Place, but even relative newcomers are proud of their unique street. Ben Wolf, a film director and director of photography, known for his work on *Obit*, *Helvetica*, *Objectified* and *The Happy Film*, moved to Dennet Place a few years ago. He purchased a New York City government photograph of the street in the 1940s, which hangs on his wall. Such tax photographs may provide the first clue as to the origin of the hobbit doors, as some homes show wooden staircases in lieu of the concrete.

Wolf surmises that residents might originally have walked under the wooden staircase, down a few steps to a door that led directly into the house. Today, the miniature doors lead to exactly that – once you enter (crouching, of course) and go down a few small steps, you can stand at full height. Make a quick left turn at the landing, down another couple of steps and there is another door that leads directly into the basement unit of the house.

It is known that the houses on Dennet Place were built for workers constructing the Catholic church St. Mary Star of the Sea on the same block between 1853 and 1855. Fans of mob history might know that this is the church where Al Capone was married.

Among Dennet Place's other mysteries is its name. On street signs, Dennet is spelled with one 'T', but in the New York City Department of Buildings records, there are two. Meanwhile, an 1860 atlas of Brooklyn shows the street name as "Bennett Place," likely named after a prominent Brooklyn family. It is believed that over the years, as in the case of other Brooklyn streets, accidental misspellings became permanent.

Regardless of its origins, the mid-block alley, itself a curious urban phenomenon in this area, retains much of its charm, and is a discovery that continues to impress even the most seasoned New Yorkers.

COUGH TRIANGLE

28

A pocket park with one tree and one shrub only, and a curious name

Triangle Park bounded by Hamilton Avenue, Court Street and Garnet Street

At the intersection of Court Street and the Brooklyn Queens Expressway/Gowanus Parkway in Carroll Gardens sits a little traffic triangle that's part of New York City's Greenstreets program. Officially called "Cough Triangle," this strangely named (see below), 0.03-acre park even has its own listing on the New York City Department of Parks website.

Cough Triangle is technically categorized as a triangle/plaza within the New York City Parks system. The parcel was first acquired by the City of New York in 1940 under the auspices of Robert Moses, the New York City Commissioner of Parks much maligned today for his urban renewal plans and expressway initiatives. Cough Triangle was transferred to the Parks Department in 1942.

When it was added as a Greenstreets site under Mayor Rudolph Guiliani, $5,000 was spent on renovation and it now features a few benches and landscaping. Parks Commissioner Henry Stern is credited with coming up with the name, one among many whimsical gestures he bestowed on newly created green spaces.

Ironically, most of Cough Triangle remains surfaced with concrete and Belgian block bricks. In a little, ill-maintained mini triangle, a tree and a shrub reside. Until a few years ago, remnant rails of a former Court Street trolley line could also be spotted on Garnet Street, though they have since been paved over.

A similarly named, but less evocative street in Brooklyn that also takes its name from surrounding streets is Triangle Three Sixteen in South Park Slope.

Court Street provides the C-O-U, Garnet provides the G, and the H comes from Hamilton Avenue

Some residents joke that Cough Triangle is named after the pollution produced by the elevated Brooklyn Queens Expressway, but it's actually named for the surrounding streets. Court Street provides the C-O-U, Garnet provides the G, and the H comes from Hamilton Avenue. The name of Court Street itself is a reference to the Kings County Courthouse, built in 1861 when Brooklyn was its own municipality. Hamilton Avenue is named after Alexander Hamilton, America's first Secretary of the Treasury, made a popular hero today through the Broadway musical by Lin-Manuel Miranda.

SHIPWRECKED MINIATURE GOLF

The only miniature golf course in New York City

621 Court Street
Brooklyn, NY 11231
718-852-4653
www.shipwreckednyc.com
Daily except Wednesdays. Opening hours vary, check website

Located in Red Hook, Shipwrecked is the only miniature golf course in New York City – and it's a fantastical one at that. The pirate-themed 18-hole course is hidden on the second floor of an industrial brick building.

The 11,000 square foot space at 621 Court Street was an open canvas, having never previously been leased to anyone, says Ryan Powers, co-owner of Shipwrecked. The architectural course is split into themes, some which reference Brooklyn's own cultural heritage, such as the Coney Island freak show, the Brooklyn Bridge and a subway station and car. There's also an underwater-themed area.

The two owners of Shipwrecked are theater majors who both hail from Ohio. Finding the hours and lifestyle on Broadway unsustainable with their young families, they channeled two of their passions – theater and mini golf – and built Shipwrecked over the course of a year. Everything inside is hand built, with special attention paid to recycling and reuse. The holes, for example, were purchased from a mini golf course in Maryland and would have otherwise gone to landfill. The pallets on which building items were delivered were reused as counters, decor, and even as the exterior structure for vintage video games.

Visitors can purchase bags of gold coins that unlock special effects and obstacles throughout the course – and the effects don't always repeat one after another, making multiple visits (or go-arounds) a must. The gold coins can even activate holograms, showcased effectively in the pirate ship lair at the beginning of the course.

Don't miss the roof of Shipwrecked where you can get a great view of the Red Hook Grain Terminal, one of the remnants of the Erie Canal projects in New York State.

THE GOWANUS BAY TERMINAL

A remnant of the Erie Canal

80 Halleck Street
Brooklyn, NY 11231
www.gowanusbayterminal.com
The interior has been opened up for the annual Open House New York Weekend
Transport: B57 to Lorraine Street/Clinton Street

A long the Henry Street Basin in Red Hook is an active reminder of Brooklyn's working waterfront. Though the Gowanus Bay Terminal (popularly known as the Grain Elevator or the Red Hook Grain Terminal) looms tall, its molding, decaying exterior reveals little of its industrial heyday.

The Gowanus Bay Terminal was a critical part of the historic New York State Barge Canal, the system that includes the Erie Canal, the Oswego Canal, the Cayuga-Seneca Canal, and the Champlain Canal. In fact, if you were wondering why a park and other places in Red Hook are named after the Erie Basin, this is why. As part of the canal project, the State of New York constructed a series of freight sheds, harbor terminals and grain elevators. The entire canal system is listed on the National Register of Historic Places, though the Gowanus Bay Terminal and other similar ones are not.

The Gowanus Bay Terminal was built in 1922 atop a tidal salt marsh, hailed as the world's largest canal terminal in Popular Mechanics. It had the latest in technological advancements, including conveyor systems and a concrete grain elevator with a capacity of 2 million bushels. The facility had 54 silos inside and could process between 25,000 incoming and 50,000 outgoing bushels per hour.

With dredging, the terminal was able to accommodate more than 200 river and ocean vessels. It was hoped that the terminal would lower the cost of transporting grain to a price per bushel last seen before World War I, a feat thought possible due to the scientific technologies applied to the design.

With the decline of the grain industry in New York, the terminal never fulfilled its expected capacity. The grain terminal loaded the last bushel in 1965, but the entire grain industry in New York had been in a period of decline for decades before. For years, the Gowanus Bay Terminal was a popular spot for urban explorers and is a frequently used location in New York City television shoots. Quadrozzi Urban Enterprises, the firm that owns the terminal, has been revitalizing and expanding the use of the facility, rebranded as GBX. Its primary aim is the "continuance of its historical bulk handling operations." Instead of grain, the facility stores and handles lumber, scrap metal, rock salt, cement powder and more. Companies at GBX include Van Line Bunkering, which receives and delivers fuels to ships like the Queen Mary II, and NYCEMCO, the city's oldest cement company. Transportation by water helps keeps trucks off the city's roads and keeps Red Hook as a working waterfront.

THE WATERFRONT MUSEUM & SHOWBOAT BARGE

Last railroad barge still floating

290 Conover Street
Brooklyn, NY 11231
Public boat tours on Saturday 1pm–5pm and Thursday 4pm–8pm
Free entry
Transport: B61 bus to Beard Street/Van Brunt Street or B57 to Dwight Street/
Van Dyck Street

To get to Pier 44 Waterfront Garden in Red Hook, you must first walk through a parking lot. At the entrance, there's a red wooden mailbox in the shape of a barge boat. Look a little further back and you'll see the original docked at the pier. This is the Waterfront Museum & Showboat Barge, a performance space and museum run by former circus performer David Sharps.

The renovated Lehigh Valley Railroad Barge No.79 was built in 1914 at the Perth Amboy Dry Dock. It's the only surviving all-wooden example of this type of barge (that once delivered coffee, rice, sugar, and other important goods) that is still accessible to the public.

These types of boats were used for over a century, from the 1860s to the 1980s, forming an important water link between large cargo ships and rail terminals. The goods on the Lehigh Valley would be loaded by stevedores onto railroad cars that would head up into northern New Jersey, eastern Pennsylvania and upstate New York. At its peak, there were possibly over 5,000 of these barges operating in New York harbor, but they became obsolete with the containerization of the shipping industry.

In 1993, Sharps acquired the covered barge for $1 and rescued it from the mud flats near the George Washington Bridge. Many of these barges were left in the shallow waters alongside abandoned railroad properties. The Lehigh Valley No.79 was sold first at a railroad auction and used for storage, allowing the structure to remain virtually unaltered. The barge, listed on the national Register of Historic Places, features many original furnishings, including a bookshelf, berth with mattress, table, stool and closet.

Barge captains lived on board, either single or with their families, and the work/life situation was especially conducive for young immigrant families. Sharps has spent a lifetime living and working on the water, from a houseboat along the Seine in Paris to commercial cruise ships. He and his family have also lived in the cabins below since 1994.

There used to be a portico atop the barge, used as additional living space, but it was removed long before Sharps got the barge, when hydraulic lifts replaced the stevedores. As a result, large support beams in the middle of the barge were taken out, which makes for a great performance space today.

Inside the barge, there are many artifacts from the Lehigh Valley Railroad, from wooden signs to longshoremen paddles. There is a great collection of gongs and bells that were once used on the barge system, sitting side by side with art pieces on display. Temporary exhibitions and a large variety of performances, ranging from circus, to opera, to theater, and more, take place on the barge, with an emphasis on waterfront history.

THE ROBOTIC CHURCH

Looking at nature at the simplest level

111 Pioneer Street
Brooklyn, NY 11231
www.facebook.com/RoboticChurchNewYork/
Open for performances a few times a year by appointment
Transport: F/G to Smith-9th Street or B61 bus to Van Brunt Street/Verona Street

Truly a secret gem, there's nothing at street level to suggest that there's an incredible site-specific installation and workshop inside this former Norwegian Seamans Church in Red Hook. Metal gates are perpetually rolled down on this brick building that dates to the 1880s. Only a doorbell next to the locked alley door gives some clue: it says "Amorphic Robotic Works".

The Robotic Church is open for performances a few times a year – the rest of the time it functions as the workshop for Amorphic Robotic Works, a collective of artists, engineers, technicians and programmers founded by Chico MacMurtie in 1991. MacMurtie is acclaimed for his large-scale, kinetic sculptures and was most recently awarded a Guggenheim fellowship for the construction of inflatable bridges that can reach across the United States-Mexico border.

While inflatables are the evolution of MacMurtie's exploration in kinetic mechanical movement, the pneumatic robots are the origin. In the Robotic Church, fifty "humanoid performers" are positioned throughout the former church nave. There's a control tower up top, through which MacMurtie can lead the performance. He tells us that the performance is "a story of their evolution," and in many ways, the evolution of humankind, "going back to the very beginning." A clocking mechanism sets the timing of the performance (usually between 40 and 60 minutes) and the robots communicate through rhythm using body language and sound. MacMurtie describes the Robotic Church performance as "looking at nature at the simplest level."

The robots range in size from 12 inches to 15 feet. They're located on multiple levels of the church, a deliberate reference to the placement of religious saints in a chapel. One robot, attached to a rope, is imbued with the objective to reach the top. Guests sit on wooden benches, "as if coming to church," MacMurtie describes.

When not activated, between three and a dozen people work in the space, testing materials and pushing the boundaries of architectural structures. In an era where popular technology is pushing ever towards virtual reality, Amorphic Robotic Works uses analog technology to explore the human condition. Instead of getting sucked into a digital world, the kinetic sculptures remind us of what it means to be alive.

THE *MARY A. WHALEN*

The last oil tanker of her kind in the U.S.

Pier 11, Atlantic Basin
Brooklyn, NY 11231
Contact via website
www.portsidenewyork.org
Deck open May to September, Monday–Friday 10am—6pm, second Sundays
5pm–12am. Interior open during public TankerTours. Group and school visits
by appointment
Transport: NYC Ferry to Red Hook or bus B61 to Van Brunt St/Verona St

The Red Hook waterfront remains an active working waterfront, with historic basins like the Erie Basin and the Henry Street Basin continuing to serve local and regional industry. At the Atlantic Basin, located just behind the Red Hook NYC Ferry stop, is the *Mary A. Whalen*, a coastal oil tanker that was launched in 1938.

Originally named the *S.T. Kiddoo*, the ship delivered oil along the Eastern Seaboard. She was originally owned by local Red Hook company Ira S. Bushey & Sons, and is the last oil tanker of her kind in the United States. The *Mary A. Whalen* also figured prominently in a significant maritime Supreme Court case in 1975.

The *Mary A. Whalen* is 172 feet long and weighs 613 gross tons. In her active period she delivered 8,019 barrels of fuel. She was built using lap-welding technique – where steel plates overlap one another – making her an archetypal artifact that exemplifies a transition period in the history of boat design. The tanker is listed on the National Register of Historic Places and serves today as the office of PortSide NewYork, a non-profit dedicated to "connect[ing] New Yorkers to the benefits of our waterways and ports and more fully tap the potential of our harbor."

Carolina Salguero, Founder and President of PortSide NewYork, says that not only does the organization host programs for the public, "but we're also very involved with the working waterfront. And in fact, what we're trying to do is show how to combine the working waterfront, public access, and community development. That's why we aren't [located] in a park." As such, the *Mary A. Whalen* functions as a museum, floating educational center, and cultural center.

One of its most popular events is TankerTime, when the main deck of the ship is open for games, art and lounging in the hammocks. TankerTime takes place in the evening of every second Sunday from May through September and features a Mediterranean music jam that Salguero refers to as "a community picnic meets a happening." The *Mary A. Whalen* also hosts students of all ages, runs educational programs for college professors, and serves as a training site for a painters' union. The organization hopes to create a program specific to the development of marine careers, as well as a boatbuilding workshop.

"What we hear a lot from people who find [the *Mary A. Whalen*] is 'This is amazing, this is what New York used to be like,'" says Salguero. "People who were here in the '70s and '80s find that they are identifying with it ... Partly [because] it's unusual, but it's also very free form."

Salguero says that PortSide wants "to show the people who run the city a more maritime way to revitalize the waterfront", and the staff of the organization are living, breathing exemplars of how this can be possible.

RETROFRET MUSIC SHOP

A hidden music shop specializing in "rare and bizarre instruments"

233 Butler Street
Brooklyn, NY 11217
Transport: R to Union Street

Retrofret is a music shop in Gowanus that specializes in "rare and bizarre instruments" and is a true discovery even before you enter the store. You'd never guess that this hodgepodge city block houses such a rich collection of historic instruments. To get to the shop inside 233 Butler

Street, you have to ring the buzzer to the building, go up a flight of stairs, cross over a rooftop and head for the inviting building across the way.

Steve Uhrik, owner of Retrofret, acknowledges that he's more interested in the unique than anything else. The business began as a repair shop and grew organically into a destination for vintage instruments when his clients started inquiring if he knew people who would buy their instruments.

Steve also has a real eye for vintage collectables, whether in high demand or not, and likes to add a modern spin. For example, he bought an Antonius Stradivarius case from August Gemunder & Sons when the company was going out of business. It once contained precious violins, including a Stradivarius, a Guarneri and one of Gemunder's own. Steve showcased an electric violin inside.

Walking through the shop with Steve is like walking through the history of stringed instruments. He explains that early guitars were so experimental, producers were just trying stuff and seeing what worked. Today, styles are much more standardized so you get far less aesthetic variety.

The merchandising in the store is also something to behold. There is a wall of mandolins, rows of vintage radios and a section with some of the first electric guitars. Some of the instruments, such as the harp guitars, vertical violas and decorative church basses, will surprise even seasoned classical musicians. When we visited, there was an 18th century French instrument known as the "hurdy gurdy" on display. A collectible ukulele was going for $10,000.

The building itself also has a great history – it was the first building to house ASPCA (American Society for the Prevention of Cruelty to Animals) in Brooklyn. Over the front door, there is a remnant of this prior usage – an engraving of a horse being beaten by a coach driver.

In addition, there's another hidden gem inside: the workshop of Mann & Truipiano that repairs organs for such venerable institutions like Trinity Church and Philadelphia's Wanamaker's Department Store – now Hecht's – for whom the firm repaired the world's largest organ.

MOSAIC HOUSE

"I thought: I can't afford to paint it, so I'll just put a flower over here. And then I couldn't stop."

108 Wyckoff Street, Brooklyn
Transport: F and G trains/Bergen St

It's curious that in New York, where a strong personality is practically compulsory, very few people personalize their house. On Wyckoff Street in Boerum Hill, you can see rows of identical brick three-stories built in the 1860s. One has come to be called the Mosaic House, and you'll know why when you see it. The entire bottom, from ground to windows, is decorated with colorful beads, buttons, tiles, and toys. Dotting the composition are small circular mirrors: whenever a car goes by, the house winks and sparkles.

Susan Gardner, a retired plastic arts professor, is the owner of the house and creator of the mosaic. A friendly woman with a quick sense of humor, Gardner gives the impression – from the barnacled outside of her home, to the museum of paintings and personal exotica inside, to her mass of curly hair and clear eye – of someone who has lived without any checks at all on the creative impulse. Asked if there exists any object that she won't cement to the front of her house, she laughs: "Absolutely not."

Standing outside, hugging herself in the cold, she tells the story. "They used to all be painted different colors," she says of the houses on the street. "Then here we were with all of them stripped down to the brick. So I came out one day and looked at our house, and the paint was peeling – a little shabby, you know, not quite keeping up with the Joneses. And I thought: I can't afford to paint it, so I'll just put a flower over here. And then I couldn't stop."

Gardner's house has by now left the Joneses for a completely different galaxy. At the same time, it has come to define the block. "People give me stuff to put on," Gardner says. "Leftovers from tiling jobs. Children leave toys that they've outgrown." She pauses. "They also *take* things."

As far as the permissibility of turning your home into public art, Gardner shrugs. "It's our house. You know, I'm at that age when I start to think about these things: at the point at which I do shuffle off, they'll probably strip the thing off. I don't see it as permanent. It's just a marking of time."

WARREN PLACE

The dawn of affordable housing

Off Warren Street, between Henry and Hicks Streets, Brooklyn
Transport: F and G trains/Bergen St; 2, 3, 4 and 5 trains/Borough Hall;
N and R trains/Court St

I n Cobble Hill, within hearing distance of the constant whoosh of the Brooklyn-Queens Expressway, there is a beguiling street – actually, a well-tended garden pathway – that is lined on both sides by connected brick buildings. This kind of arrangement is usually called a mews, but the term refers to a collection of converted stables, whereas Warren Place's houses, while tiny (only 11-feet-wide, close to the New York City record for smallness) were made to be lived in. Built in 1878, they were once the avant-garde in affordable housing.

The visionary who built Warren Place was a native Brooklynite named Alfred Tredway White. Son of a wealthy importer, White was active in education and got his first close look at urban poverty while visiting the families of students in their homes. He discovered that comfortable living conditions don't just reflect prosperity: they create it. The chief evils were the lack of ventilation and light of New York tenements, which at the time were hothouses for cockroaches, tuberculosis, emphysema, and nameless malaise. Instead White offered, through various housing projects, sunlight, open air, a sense of community, modern amenities like running water and plumbing, and dignity. The dignity worked both ways: White's motto was "philanthropy plus 5%," 5% being the return he promised his investors.

It worked. "Mr. White never has any trouble with his tenants, though he gathers in the poorest," said Jacob Riis, one of the city's greatest advocates of adequate housing. "They are like a big village of contented people, who live in peace with one another." Although the ghost of White grimaces at the irony, perhaps the greatest testament to the success of Warren Place is what the properties are worth today. "It was purposefully done for the workers," says Douglas, who owns the corner house on the southwest side. "Now it's, you know, million-dollar homes."

Warren Place was more than half a century ahead of the curve. The New York City Housing Authority wasn't founded until 1934; a couple of years later the first city-financed residences for low-income families were built in the Lower East Side.

Down south

BROOKLYN VISITATION MONASTERY

An active monastery, open to the curious

8202 Ridge Blvd.Brooklyn, NY 11209
www.brooklynvisitationmonastery.org
Transport: R to 86 Street

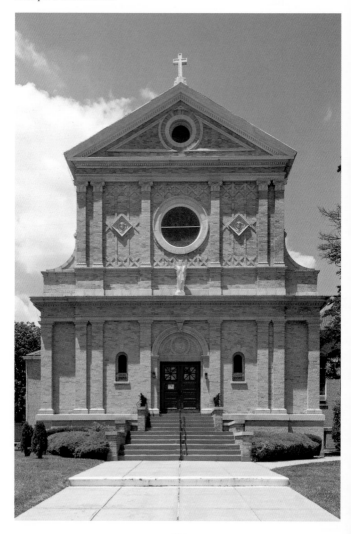

In the heart of Bay Ridge, the Brooklyn Visitation Monastery is an active cloister, home to the Sisters of the Order of the Visitation of Holy Mary, an order founded in Annecy, France in 1610. The Brooklyn monastery was founded in 1855. According to their website, any woman can take a weekend retreat there on the 7.5 acre enclosed campus if they have "ever wondered what monastic life is like" – just call the monastery and speak to the Retreat Directress.

The monastery itself is surrounded by 22 foot walls, but an Italianate church, an all-girls Catholic school and the Brooklyn Visitation Academy are open to the street. Inside the enclosed portion there are several multi-level buildings, a pond known as St. Mary's Lake and forested open space. A rare video of the buildings showed vaulted hallways and a plethora of sculptures both inside and outside.

After an initial formation period, the full process of joining the monastery takes about six years to the final vows. Unlike the stricter Carmelite Monastery in Cypress Hills, the Brooklyn Visitation Monastery openly discusses the activities of the monastery on its website via the sisters' blog. Daily tasks include gardening, cooking and working in the infirmary. Exercise is another important activity; the nuns cycle, play basketball and volleyball. Paddle boats are used on the lake.

Students of the Brooklyn Visitation Academy get to see the grounds of the monastery as well. There are sleigh rides in the winter and picnics when it is warm. A campus ministry program was launched at the Brooklyn Visitation Academy in 2015 to teach teenagers the importance of community service.

Artist Anne Goetze, who has captured her aunt in the Visitation Monastery in Annecy for two decades using her brush, exhibited her work at the Brooklyn Visitation Monastery in 2015. She says she wanted to capture how her aunt has affected her and how the sisters, "in their very quiet way affected others, how they affect the world in their quiet way. Their life is dedicated to prayer. I don't know anyone else that does that."

BARKALOO CEMETERY

The smallest cemetery in Brooklyn, with only two people buried in it

34 Mackay Place
Brooklyn, NY 11209
Open 24 hours – there is a gate but it does not lock
Transport: R to Bay Ridge Avenue

On the corner of Mackay Place and Narrows Avenue in Bay Ridge sits the smallest cemetery in Brooklyn, with only two people buried in it. The plot of land was purchased in 1725 by Dutch immigrant William Harmans Barkaloo as a family cemetery and is the only family cemetery independent from any larger ones in the borough.

The Barkaloos (sometimes written Barkulo) lived in the area into the 20th century. A plaque placed in 1962 at the gates dubs it the "Revolutionary War Cemetery", making the assertion that the two men buried there – Harmans (or Harms) Barkulo, the son of William, and Simon Cortelyou – fought on the side of the Patriots at the Battle of Brooklyn during the American Revolution. Both tombstones state that the two fought in the New York Militia, with Harmans Barkulo serving as a lieutenant. Cortelyou ended up in the Barkaloo Cemetery because he married the widow of Jacques Barkaloo.

Cortelyou's great-great grandfather was the famous Dutch surveyor Jacques Cortelyou, after whom the Brooklyn road was named. Jacques settled in New Amsterdam in 1652, was appointed as Surveyor General, and created the earliest known map of the Dutch settlement, now known as the Castello plan. He also founded the settlement of New Utrecht, which is now the area of Bensonhurst in Brooklyn.

Carol Inskeep, author of *The Graveyard Shift: A Family Historian's Guide to New York City Cemeteries*, writes that "The Cortelyou family, who owned the land, allowed the ground to be used as a graveyard for some 60 soldiers who died during the battle," including possibly those that belonged to the Stillwell, Suydam and Ward families. Some believe that some of the headstones were taken to use as doorsteps and that some of the bodies were moved to other cemeteries later.

The monument standing in the cemetery was unveiled in 1976, an initiative of Robert I. Porter from the Veteran of Foreign Wars Post 985. Nonetheless, there has been some debate as to true extent of the Revolutionary War connections. There is some evidence that the Cortelyous were, in fact, Loyalists or, at best, neutral during the war. Whatever the truth may be, the last burial at Barkaloo Cemetery was in 1848 and it remains fairly well-maintained to this day.

LOST STATEN ISLAND RAILWAY ③

A never-finished tunnel to Staten Island

Owl's Head Park
68 Colonial Road
Brooklyn, NY 11220
Transport: R to Bay Ridge Avenue

In 1923, Mayor John F. Hylan broke ground on a passenger and freight rail tunnel that would have connected Bay Ridge with the St. George Ferry Terminal on Staten Island. It was to be known as the

Brooklyn-Richmond Freight and Passenger Tunnel. The project never came to fruition but buried 150 feet below Owl's Head Park today are the shaft and tunnel, which still remain. Another shaft was sunk at St. George's Ferry but was filled in with the redevelopment of the terminal in 1946. The story has been mostly lost to history but there is a stone on the western side of Owl's Head Park that is believed to mark the entrance to the lost tunnel.

In Brooklyn the tunnel would have connected to the Long Island Railroad's Bay Ridge Division. According to a 1964 newspaper article, the tunnel would link railroads west and east of the Hudson River to continuous freight by rail. If it had been built, it would have been the longest tunnel of its type ever constructed, "and the equal of the largest," reported *The New York Times* in 1924.

Although there were plans to build a subway tunnel along this route as well, the schematic that was put into action in 1923 was for rail and freight only. In addition, the 1964 article explains, "There were supposed to be passenger stations along the new line and separate subway tunnels were to be built later, when passenger traffic reached such a volume that they could be justified. It was not intended to connect this tunnel directly to the BMT Fourth Avenue line."

In 1921, there was another plan to build a tunnel to Greenville, New Jersey, put forth by The Port Authority of New York and New Jersey under Governor Al Smith. But Mayor Hylan dismissed the plan, which would have competed with his own. He claimed it was "an absolute joke. It is impractical and will never be completed."

In 1924, Hylan's plans were halted by the passage of the Nicoll-Hofstadter Act by none other than Governor Smith. The act prevented the tunnels under construction to be used for freight. Hylan's plans

were declared "at variance with the comprehensive port plan," reported *The New York Times* that year.

In the end Hylan was right about the Port Authority tunnel — it never got built (although an active route for freight runs by barge between Brooklyn and Greenville, New Jersey today). Over the years, plans to restart the tunnel project resurfaced in other proposals but none came to fruition.

RAIL TRAINS AT THE 65TH STREET RAIL YARD ④

Floating train barge to Jersey

Leif Ericson Drive
Brooklyn, NY 11220
Transport: N/R to 59th Street

Just south of the Brooklyn Army Terminal in Sunset Park is one of New York City's infrastructure survivors: a floating barge freight train line that runs from the 65th Street Rail Yard to Jersey City across the Hudson River. The New York New Jersey Rail, founded in 2005, is operated now by the Port Authority of New York and New Jersey. Although the line is only four miles long, it serves as a small, but increasingly critical link for freight in the New York region, and cements the city's commitment to bringing industry back to the waterfront.

"We're an anomaly. Out of the 500 railroads in the United States, the nearest one that looks like us in texture and feel is the Alaska railroad," says Donald B. Hutton, Managing Director of the New York and New Jersey Rail. The Port Authority bought the floating rail line in 2008 and the NYC Economic Development Corporation rebuilt the rail yard itself, which reopened in 2012. But many different railroads and companies have operated this line in the past, including the Pennsylvania Railroad. The last iteration, the New York Cross Harbor Railroad, moved much of the country's cocoa.

The ride takes 35 to 40 minutes. The floats transport 14 train cars at once (the equivalent of 56 semi-trucks) on two tracks side by side, although the Port Authority is currently building new car floats that will have four tracks, accommodating 18 train cars (equivalent to 72 trucks) and providing faster unload and reload times.

New York and New Jersey Rail transports a large amount of local lumber and building materials, as well as food products like soybean oil, Washington state apples, separated recycled materials from the nearby SIMS Municipal Recycling Facility and other solid waste like scrap metal. Special cargo has included New York City transit subway cars and oversize pieces for the Willis Avenue Bridge, which spans the Harlem River.

There are two timber and steel float bridges, built in 2000, which are modern versions of the transfer bridges and gantries you still see around the New York waterfront. A locomotive pushes the freight cars onto the barge and a tugboat pulls the floating barge across the harbor, where it reaches another lift bridge and gets locked to it via a series of pins.

More than 90 per cent of goods in the New York region are moved by truck, with only 2 per cent of New York City served by freight rail. The only other option to move freight by rail across the Hudson River is over a bridge 140 miles north of New York City – a three-day trip by rail. In 2016, New York New Jersey Rail moved about 3,400 railcars across the Hudson. But with an expansion in progress, the line will have a capacity of 24,000 rail cars per year. With freight transportation predicted to to double by 2030, this sole rail link across the Hudson River will be more important than ever.

WORLD WAR II GUARD TOWERS AT BROOKLYN ARMY TERMINAL

Towers that once protected New York

140 58th Street
Brooklyn, NY 11220
Accessible on special tours run by Untapped Cities
Transport: N/R to 59th Street

Situated at the southern edge of Sunset Park, along the Brooklyn waterfront, the Brooklyn Army Terminal is a 4 million square foot structure built between 1918 and 1919. It was the largest concrete building in the world when it was completed. As an indicator of the importance of this complex, architect Cass Gilbert, who designed the Woolworth Building, United States Supreme Court in Washington D.C. and the U.S. Customs House in Manhattan, was hired for the project.

The facility was the main depot and supply base for the American troops fighting in Europe during the end of World War I but was most active during World War II, when 20,000 people were employed at the facility.

One of the little known secrets of the Brooklyn Army Terminal is the function of the four protruding miniature buildings atop both building A and building B. These were built as guard towers and were manned during World War II. Today, the towers are filled with pigeon carcasses and old newspapers. The rooftops are not usually open to the public, but are accessible on tours run by *Untapped Cities*, in partnership with the New York City Economic Development Corporation.

The Brooklyn Army Terminal was decommissioned in 1957. Purchased by the city in 1981, the complex began a multi-decade renovation into office space and manufacturing uses – a process that is ongoing. The most stunning space of the terminal is the multi-level atrium in building B with its staggered balconies. Cranes would pick up palettes from the trains, lift them up and drop them directly to a balcony above. A Long Island Railroad train sits on the tracks to give a sense of what the space was like when freight was driven directly into the building. Today, part of that track area has been converted into an indoor lobby.

Some of the sky bridges, which connect buildings A and B, remain in a raw, untouched state, awaiting future renovation.

Brooklyn Army Terminal originally had 96 elevators, the largest capacity for freight elevators in the world when built. It was also the largest military supply base in the world through the end of World War II and held a record in the Book of World Records for how much concrete was mixed and poured in a day.

Where Elvis boarded for Europe during WWII

During WWII, the Brooklyn Army Terminal also served as an embarkation point for troops heading to Europe. The most famous of these soldiers was Elvis, who arrived by train directly onto the pier. He gave two press conferences then boarded the ship he would take across the Atlantic.

FAITH MOSQUE

A mosque in an old movie theater

5911 Eighth Avenue, Brooklyn
718-438-6919
www.fatihcami.org
Friday service is at 11:30am; come at 2pm at the earliest for visits, otherwise call
Transport: N train/8th Av

The neighborhood of Sunset Park has the largest population of Chinese in New York outside of Chinatown and an even larger Hispanic population. A walk there offers a heavy dose of the city's cultural warp, and on Eighth Avenue you can explore an even deeper level: a warp within the warp. Push through the door at number 5911, remove your shoes, and pass into a shining interior of cool blue. It's the prayer hall of the Fatih Mosque.

It's a little like walking into an indoor pool. The geometry is plain: a carpeted floor with no chairs, and in the east wall the smooth alcove that indicates the direction of Mecca (*mihrab*) and the elevated pulpit (*minbar*). But here it's the details that sing. The walls are sheathed in tile: glossy floral patterns, cobalt blocks with calligraphic messages in white. Each tile was made in Turkey. "From a place called Kütahya," says Mesud, one of Fatih's imams. "It's a very famous place for tiles."

This dazzle of Islamic culture within the most Chinese neighborhood of Brooklyn is even odder given the building's history: it was once the Berkshire Theatre, a movie house. History has a sense of humor about this: according to Making Muslim Space in North America and Europe by Barbara Metcalf, the Berkshire's decorating theme was "a Hollywood amalgam of Orientalist-Moorish-Arabesque fantasies". The mihrab and minbar are now against what used to be the theater's back wall: seated moviegoers once faced exactly the other way. The mosque, in other words, turned fake Islam into real, and flipped the whole direction in the process. It's a re-Orientation within a reorientation. The theme goes a little further: Muslim worshippers "literally turn their backs," writes Metcalf, "on the space where sex goddesses were once displayed on the screen, which is instead now occupied by women screened off from view."

Sounds exciting. But nobody in the congregation is looking to make this point. When asked how the worshippers here feel about praying in a former movie theater, imam Mesud squints. "I don't think they know," he says.

> Before becoming mostly Chinese, the neighborhood around Fatih Mosque was an unlikely mix of Middle Eastern, Asian, and Scandinavian.

SITE OF THE RED LION INN

*Where the Battle of Brooklyn
and the American Revolution began*

4th Avenue and 35th Street entrance to Green-Wood Cemetery
Cemetery open daily, hours seasonal
Transport: D/N/R to 36th Street

In a forgotten little outcrop of Green-Wood Cemetery, accessed through a gate on 4th Avenue and 35th Street, a plaque marks the site of the former Red Lion Inn. The opening shots of the Battle of Brooklyn, the first battle of the American Revolution, were fired here.

The plaque, presented by the citizens of the state of Delaware and the Delaware Regiment, reads:

"Outnumbered four to one, and nearly encircled, Stirling ordered the Delaware Regiment to make a fighting retreat. With colors flying they made an orderly withdrawal, and against great odds, crossed Gowanus Creek, to safety. Following the battle the regiment's commander reported two men killed and 24 missing, being captured, killed, or drowned during crossing. Noted for its discipline and bravery, the Delaware Regiment continued to serve with distinction throughout the war."

On August 27, 1776, in a push towards capturing Brooklyn Heights, the British attacked American pickets defending the Red Lion Inn, commencing the Battle of Brooklyn. Brooklyn Heights was considered an important defensive holding for the City of New York. The Americans were pushed back up Gowanus Road, from where they were assisted by Brigadier General William Alexander Lord Stirling, the Delaware Regiment and the famous Maryland 400. The American pickets from the Red Lion found safety in Brooklyn Heights.

The inn was situated at the junction of three country roads: Martense Lane, the Narrows Road, and Gowanus Road. The first two are still noted with vintage street signs in the same style as the rest of Green-Wood Cemetery's many paths. The Gowanus Road was a key colonial road that enabled the retreat of George Washington's troops. Alas, there is no record of what the Red Lion Inn looked like, but it was likely built

of wood in a similar style to other roadside country inns on Long Island. Today, the site contains maintenance facilities and a garage, alongside existing gravestones.

Green-Wood Cemetery has a long-term goal to renovate the maintenance facilities, but as yet there are no concrete plans in place.

THE CATACOMBS
OF GREEN-WOOD CEMETERY

Family vaults built into a hill

500 25th Street
Brooklyn, NY 11232
www.green-wood.com
Cemetery open daily, hours seasonal
Catacombs opened up on special tours, members' events and usually for Open House New York weekend (see website for schedule)
Transport: D/N/R to 25th Street

Opened to the public only once or twice a year for special events, the catacombs are probably the most elusive spot in Green-Wood Cemetery.

Access is gained using an old-fashioned dungeon-like key, which unlocks the iron gates out front. The staff of Green-Wood Cemetery calls the space "30 Vaults," a reference to the number of vaults inside.

Located underneath a hill that stretches for about 150 feet, the catacombs date to the early 1850s and were built into an area of the cemetery that was mined for gravel. According to Green-Wood Cemetery historian Jeff Richman, they were a "sort of apartment house for above ground interment ... a middle class option for people who wanted the luxury of above ground interment without the expense of constructing something on [their] own."

The most famous person buried in the catacombs is Ward McAllister, the Gilded Age high society tastemaker who coined the term "The 400" when referring to the exclusive set in New York City that could fit in Mrs. Astor's ballroom. He was not as wealthy or blue-blooded as those he advised, so burial in the Green-Wood catacombs was a worthy achievement for someone of his stature. Richman says McAllister would have been "quite chagrined to know that the catacombs are now locked up and that access is very limited." However, the McAllister family vault is the only one marked by a special historical plaque.

One of the "greatest tourist destinations in America" in the 1850s

The 478 acres of Green-Wood Cemetery are so packed with history it would take days to see it all. Among the most famous of the 560,000 buried here include Michel Basquiat, Leonard Bernstein, Boss Tweed, and many more notable New Yorkers.

Founded in 1838, Green-Wood Cemetery was the first of the rural cemeteries in New York City, designed with rolling hills, bucolic scenery, and stunning views out to New York harbor.

According to Richman, it was one of the "greatest tourist destinations in America" with half a million people a year visiting by the 1850s. Today, the visitors are fewer, though the buried are more.

THE MCGOVERN-WEIR GREENHOUSE

The only Victorian greenhouse still standing in NYC

Corner of Fifth Avenue and 25th Street
Brooklyn, NY 11232
Transport: D/N/R to 25th Street

Across from Green-Wood Cemetery's Fifth Avenue and 25th Street entrance is a magnificent little greenhouse, sitting incongruously next to a gas station and warehouses, topped with a vintage style sign that reads "McGovern-Weir".

In 2011, when reporting on its potential sale, *The New York Times* called it the "small, private counterpart to the great conservatories in Brooklyn and the Bronx." In 1982, preservationist Andrew Dolkart wrote in the landmarks designation report for the greenhouse that it was the "rarest of nineteenth-century survivors" and that it was "the only surviving commercial Victorian greenhouse in all of New York City."

Made of glass, copper, wrought iron and wood, the McGovern-Weir Greenhouse was built in 1895 by architect G. Curtis Gillespie, replacing a similar earlier structure. By all accounts, it was a destination in itself, with its high domed roofs, bays and delicate Victorian details.

James Weir, the original owner, is buried at Green-Wood Cemetery. Kay McGovern bought the greenhouse in 1971 but it was still in operation under her son until at least 1982, after which it was not continuously maintained. Still, even in a decayed state, it was easy to imagine the greenhouse overflowing with flowers in its heyday.

In February 2012, Green-Wood Cemetery acquired the property for $1.625 million after several years of negotiation with the intention to renovate and reuse the greenhouse as a visitors center, exhibition gallery and event space. The cemetery also acquired some of the buildings next door, which have been demolished, and plans to construct a new building to host offices, archives, and publicly accessible spaces.

In January 2013, Green-Wood was awarded a $500,000 grant by New York State's Regional Economic Development Council to restore the greenhouse. The first step of the restoration was an architectural study which was completed in 2013. After that the restoration began, with additional funding through a New York City grant.

The complicated restoration process has involved deconstructing the greenhouse and putting it back together, retaining original elements where possible. At the time of publication, wrought iron rehabilitation was completed, the walls had been reconstructed with both original and new bricks, and the copper domes were reconstructed. The windows, made of swamp Cyprus wood frames, were fabricated "as close as we could replicate to the original," says Eric Barna, Vice-President of Operations at Green-Wood Cemetery. The greenhouse is expected to reopen in spring 2019.

THE "CIVIC VIRTUE TRIUMPHANT OVER UNRIGHTEOUSNESS" STATUE

The most hated statue in New York City

Inside Green-Wood Cemetery
500 25th Street
Brooklyn, NY 11232
Cemetery open daily, hours seasonal
Transport: D/N/R to 25th Street

At the end of 2012, Green-Wood Cemetery accepted one of the most controversial statues in New York City history. The statue "Civic Virtue Triumphant Over Unrighteousness" once stood in City Hall Park as part of a fountain. Installed in 1922, the allegorical piece was commissioned in 1909. It's importance as a municipal work was so great that the City of New York actually took out an insurance policy on the life of its sculptor, Frederick MacMonnies. His $60,000 commission, if valued in 1909 dollars would today be equivalent to $1.6 million.

The sculpture, lauded as the largest sculpture ever made by an American, was constructed in MacMonnies' atelier in Normandy, France. It was buried twice during World War I, first in Normandy and later in Paris, to protect it from the Germans.

The 22-ton statue, carved from a single block of marble, is meant to represent the triumph of virtue over corruption and vice. The only problem: the nearly naked male figure is triumph, towering and dominating over two female mermaids representing corruption and vice. Women found this misogynist and offensive; even men thought it looked like the virtue was kicking or trampling the female figures.

By 1929, James J. Walker, the Commissioner of Public Works was calling the sculpture "the Fat Boy standing in a mass of worms" and advocating for its removal. By 1932, still nothing had happened: new locations all across the city were considered for the statue, but *The New York Herald Tribune* worried that no other borough would volunteer to "carry the marble titan away from the bereaved borough of Manhattan."

The statue was finally moved in 1941 at the request of Queens Borough President George U. Harvey: its arrival lending some pomp to the opening of the new Queens Borough Hall. Mayor Fiorello LaGuardia was also happy about it, stating, "Oh, it's gone at last. Now I won't have to look at that virtuous back any more."

Due to the long-standing controversy, the statue had been denied conservation in the 71 years it stood in Queens: it was falling apart and the fountain had long stopped working. Anthony Weiner even suggested selling the statue on Craigslist. But in 2011, Green-Wood President Richard J. Moylan offered to give the statue a home in the cemetery, and by early 2013, "Civic Virtue" was placed among other statues by sculptors contemporary to MacMonnies, such as Daniel Chester French and John Quincy Adams Ward.

THE LOCATION
OF MINERVA STATUE

Built with a view to the Statue of Liberty

Battle Hill, inside Green-Wood Cemetery
500 25th Street
Brooklyn, NY 11232
Cemetery open daily, hours seasonal
Transport: D/N/R to 25th Street

With a total of 50,000 soldiers, the Battle of Brooklyn was the first battle during the American Revolutionary War, and the largest until Yorktown in 1781 when the British surrendered. Because of the valiant efforts of the Maryland 400, along with many who fought to the death near the Old Stone House to allow for George Washington's retreat, and a nor'easter that delayed the arrival of British ships to New York, this defeat on the Patriot side did not begin and end the war.

Battle Hill in Green-Wood Cemetery is one of the key sites of the Battle of Brooklyn. As Jeff Richman, historian for the Green-Wood Cemetery writes, "For too long, the battle received short shrift from historians, who were uninterested in writing about what was an American defeat." But in 1920, one man sought to rectify that. In front of the plot he purchased at Green-Wood Cemetery, Charles Higgins, a notable New Yorker and the inventor of Higgins American Indian Ink, installed a bronze statue of Minerva.

At the highest natural point in Brooklyn, 200 feet above sea level, Minerva is placed deliberately with arm saluting the Statue of Liberty. This orientation would seem logical, given the symbolism of the Statue of Liberty, a gift from France to commemorate the independence of the United States.

But, as old blueprints in the Green-Wood Cemetery surveyor's office reveal, the original plan for Minerva was to have her facing the Woolworth Building in Lower Manhattan. Written on these drawings are the words "FACE N.W. TO THE WOOLWORTH BUILDING." The Woolworth Building, the tallest building in the world from 1913 to 1930, was a technological and architectural marvel. Later plans added her raised left arm and revised her orientation: "POINTING DIRECTLY TO THE STATUE OF LIBERTY".

This question of orientation came to a head in the early 2000s when the neighborhood was upzoned and a developer hoped to build a 70-foot-tall condominium at the corner of Seventh Avenue and 23rd Street. This new building would have blocked Minerva's view to the Statue of Liberty. Community groups and preservationists joined forces to protest the development. Caving to pressure, the developer signed a pact with Green-Wood stating that "persons of average height standing on the ground at the base of Minerva will still maintain an unobstructed view to the Statue of Liberty." In the plans, a notch was added to a roof corner so that Lady Liberty could be seen. The building was not completed until 2010, likely due to recession and other issues, and ended up far shorter at 40 feet.

The views remained, but Green-Wood Cemetery hoped to add requests for a view corridor in the neighborhood's official community plan.

JAPANESE TORII ATOP FORMER BISHOP FORD HIGH SCHOOL

Surprising Asian architecture

500 19th Street
Brooklyn, NY 11215

Driving along Prospect Expressway, you might notice a red *torii* – a traditional Japanese gate – sitting on the roof of a mid-century style institutional building. The building at 500 19th Street was formerly Bishop Ford High School, a Catholic school named for Francis Xavier Ford, a beloved Brooklyn-born Roman Catholic bishop who died in a Chinese communist prison in 1952 following extensive torture. Ford arrived in China in 1918, after graduating from the American Foreign Mission Society (now known as Maryknoll), and was one of the first four American Catholic priests to serve there. As a martyr, the Roman Catholic Diocese of Brooklyn has been putting forth a petition for his canonization.

Bishop Ford High School was opened in 1962 as an all-boys school and was made co-ed in 1976. The school was noted not only for the *torii* on the roof (topped by a cross), but also for its stylish interior decor that melded Eastern influences with Western architecture. Chinese-style lamps lined the grand lobby, along with red and gold painted columns. The floors of some classrooms were of red and black tile. The black pews of the chapel had touches of red paint on the ends and a red sign in front of the school used a stylized Chinese-influenced font. The *torii* reappeared here, circumscribing a Christian cross, as the logo of the school. The lampposts on the property, which still exist today, were also similarly Asian-influenced, and even the radio antenna is red. The annual yearbook was called the Pagoda, possibly inspired by the biography of Bishop Ford entitled *The Pagoda and the Cross: The Life of Bishop Ford of Maryknoll.*

The school has made some quirky appearances in pop culture: parts of the film *Dog Day Afternoon* were filmed in the school, as were the music videos for R.E.M's "All The Way to Reno (You're Going to Be a Star)," directed by Michael Moore, and Drake's "Best I Ever Had". In 2013, record producer Mike Will Make It shot a music video at Bishop Ford High School featuring himself, Miley Cyrus and Wiz Khalifa.

The site itself also has some history. The school was built on empty lots that once housed barns for the Brooklyn trolley. And a Federal prison was located on this property during the Civil War. Bishop Ford High School closed at the end of the school year in 2014, faced with declining enrollment and massive debt. In 2015, the building reopened with extensive renovation as a Universal Pre-K program, one of Mayor Bill DeBlasio's major initiatives.

Yet, the *torii* still sits on top, sans the Christian Cross, as a reminder of the building's past, as does the building's cornerstone, which reads "For God and Country".

Nameless parks in Brooklyn ⑬

As to be expected, most parks in New York City have a formal name – from grand names like Prospect Park to the very functional, like "Public Place" and the aforementioned Cough Triangle. Brooklyn has the distinction of having the highest number of nameless parks, simply labeled as "Park" in the New York City Department of Parks database. The official signs on site also simply say "PARK," which is always a rather lonely sight to behold. There are 15 "Parks" and a solo "Triangle" in Brooklyn.

Most are likely initiatives of Greenstreets (now the Green Infrastructure Unit), a partnership between the New York City Department of Parks and the Department of Transportation seeking to reclaim unused parts of the city streets and transform them into green spaces. Some are more effective than others, with developed landscaping, benches and fences. Others remain forgotten as poorly maintained patches of no-man's land.

Many of these nameless parks are centered around Windsor Terrace along Prospect Expressway and Fort Hamilton Parkway just a few blocks from Prospect Park. Others are located in Dumbo, Williamsburg, Bay Ridge, South Slope and Clinton Hill.

Geoffrey Croft, founder of New York City Park Advocates, a non-profit watchdog group, told Brooklyn Paper in 2013 that many

such parks were "certainly waiting to be named." At the same time, a spokesman for the Parks Department told the paper that "There's no single reason why a park remains unnamed" but local residents at the time were pushing for the opportunity to honor locals or name the unnamed parks after something more inspiring.

Names can be updated by a decision of the Parks commissioner or through the passage of a local law. Several years later, however, the number of nameless parks in Brooklyn has remained the same.

KENSINGTON HORSE STABLES

The only remaining stable in the Prospect Park area

11 Ocean Parkway and 51 Caton Place
Brooklyn, NY 11218
www.kensingtonstables.com
10am to sunset, lessons: call 718-972-4588

Next to a modern apartment building is a nondescript brick structure that dates to the 1930s. Look closely and you'll see that there are dozens of horses inside. Kensington Horse Stables at 51 Caton Place is the last remnant of a riding academy from the early 20th century, with this structure built as an extension of a main facility at 11 Ocean Parkway.

Prospect Park was designed by Frederick Law Olmstead and Calvert Vaux, the same landscape architects as Central Park. Like the latter, Prospect Park was meant to accommodate the horse, with bridle paths and carriage drives. The riding academy, then run by Adolph Vogt, was an important part of the new park. Vogt cut his teeth as the Riding Master and later the proprietor of the Bedford Riding Academy on Bedford and Atlantic Avenue in the Crown Heights area that would later become Automobile Row.

Automobile traffic had made Bedford Avenue inhospitable to horse riding, so in 1917 Vogt looked to expand to another location in southern Crown Heights, near the entrance to Prospect Park off of Malbone Street (now Empire Boulevard). The New York Supreme Court ruled that Vogt could not build there, so he found a new site in Windsor Terrace at 11-27 Ocean Parkway. There, he built the largest riding ring in Brooklyn, conveniently located for direct access to the bridle path to Coney Island. Since repurposed as a warehouse space, 11 Ocean Parkway still stands today ...

Nearby, Kensington Horse Stables, the only remaining stable in the Prospect Park area, still uses the building at 51 Caton Place. Under the pavement on the street you can see old Belgian blocking peeking out. A small arena inside is used for lessons, though most of the instruction is given on the Prospect Park Bridle Path. There's also an outdoor space in the back for educational programs.

Kensington Horse Stables aims to teach riders about horsemanship, or the "art of horses," – more than just horse riding, says Barbara Stork, who works at the stable. The stable focuses on developing the relationship between the rider and the horse. Each horse has its own personality, says Stork.

You can also book a carriage ride in Prospect Park through Kensington Horse Stables or rent ponies for parties and film shoots. The horse Tonka, for example, has been on Saturday Night Live, while Emma is used as a picture horse because she knows how to stay very still. The stable also participates in Gallop NYC, a therapeutic program for people with disabilities.

QUAKER CEMETERY

Burials in the park

Prospect Park, Brooklyn
Enter at Prospect Park Southwest between 11th Avenue and
Terrace Place; gate to the cemetery is on the left of Center Drive about
300 yards in
Prospect Park open daily 5am–1am

Prospect Park has a feature that distinguishes it from any other public space in the city: when you die, you can be buried there. All you have to do is be a practicing Quaker.

Although historically more associated with Queens where the religious movement first took root in New York, there are more Quakers in Brooklyn than in any other part of the state. On the map of Prospect Park, about a hundred yards in from where 11th Avenue ends, there is an area labeled: "Friends Cemetery: Private." On the ground, you might miss it: there's only one road that leads there, and it's cut off by a fence. At a recent quarterly meeting, one of the Friends — jeans, grey mustache, baseball cap — sits on a lawn chair to keep a watch on the entrance. "The gravestones go all the way up over the hill, and down again," he says. When asked how a non-Quaker might see them, he says: "Well, you just walk along the fence."

This is not easy. The chain-link, containing about 12 acres of land, runs through wild patches of maple sapling and bush. As you whack your way around, now and again you'll spy clearings within, crossed with sunlight, and marked by orderly rows of stones. The simplicity of Quaker life extends to memorials: the stones are all cut from the same model, small and squat, about the size of a shoebox. The private cemetery is also full of giant maple trees, some of them cloaked in ivy, and the feel of the place is generally denser, and greener, and more ancient than other parts of the park. This is to be expected: when Prospect was created in the 1860s, Calvert Vaux and Frederick Law Olmsted (the same wizards who designed Central Park) had to work around the small cemetery, which was already in use.

The plot has remained Quaker ever since, and burials continue today. "Around six people a year," says the Friend at the gate. "And there are already around two thousand." When asked how the rest of Brooklyn feels about the Quakers maintaining a part of the public park for their personal use, he thinks for a long moment, eyes scanning the dirt. "We've gotten some bad press along the way," he admits, "for being private and not letting people in. But they should be happy because usually it's very hard to find anything to hold against Quakers."

ERASMUS HALL ACADEMY

Stained glass treasures inside a school

911 Flatbush Avenue
Brooklyn, NY 11226
718-564-2551 or contact via website for visits
http://schools.nyc.gov/SchoolPortals/17/K539
Monday–Friday 8am–2:20pm
Transport: B/Q to Church Avenue

Nestled in the heart of Brooklyn is Erasmus Hall; one of New York City's most impressive yet little known treasures. This Gothic-style school, reminiscent of the colleges at Oxford and Cambridge, was founded in 1786 in an area settled by the Dutch. It is considered one of the oldest schools in the United States and was the first secondary school chartered by the New York State Regents. Erasmus Hall was funded by some of the country's most famous Founding Fathers, including Alexander Hamilton and Aaron Burr, and counts among its alumni such figures as Mae West, Barbra Streisand and Neil Diamond. Today, five schools use the complex now known as Erasmus Hall Educational Campus, which is filled with notable art and architecture.

Beyond the exterior architecture, the interior of the school reveals the rich history of the building. The current complex was built around

Photos by F. Frissard (left) and Sian Rice (right)

- 182 -

an original 1786 wooden clapboard school building in 1904 by school superintendent C.B.J. Snyder, who is credited with over 400 of New York City's most architecturally notable schools. Artwork was an important part of school design during Snyder's time, with most schools incorporating site-specific commissioned artworks of various mediums.

But Erasmus Hall is special; it is brimming with stained glass. The most famous piece (along with the sculptures in the garden) can be seen from the outside. However, viewed from within the vaulted two-floor auditorium, designed much like a church, it is a sight to behold. Behind the stage, *The Life of Erasmus* opulently portrays the life of the school's namesake. All through the school, traditional stained glass motifs contrast with modern imagery, including sections depicting American industry and scientific research.

Above the main entrance along Flatbush Avenue, you'll see five panels of stained glass on the second floor behind the turreted façade – a work that was created by Louis Comfort Tiffany, the son of the famous jeweler. This stained glass gem was originally commissioned for the school library in 1919 to honor the first principal of Erasmus Hall, Walter B. Gunnison. The Neoclassical subject matter shows a figure (representing knowledge) amid a Roman scene created using a combination of painted and plated glass techniques. Due to overcrowding, the library has since been converted into two classrooms but the Tiffany piece remains in situ.

THE JAPANESE HOUSE

A turn-of-the-century gem

131 Buckingham Road
Brooklyn, NY 11226
Occasional tours of the Japanese House are hosted by the Fischer family
Entry fee: Inquire at 131tour@gmail.com for dates and pricing
Transport: B/Q to Church Avenue

For those unfamiliar with Flatbush and Prospect Park South, the number of detached Victorian mansions may come as a surprise. But even for the more acquainted, the presence of a Japanese house is still extraordinary.

The Frederick and Loretta Kohle House, more popularly referred to as the "Japanese House" dates back to 1902-1903. The entire area was a speculative real estate endeavor by Dean Alvord, who wanted to build a suburban-style enclave to prove that rural beauty could be possible in an urban street grid context.

Residential architecture in America in the late 19th and early 20th centuries was heavily influenced by the success of the Japanese pavilion at the World's Columbian Exhibition in Chicago in 1893. The mansions of the elite were decorated with "Oriental rooms," filled with items imported from Asia. But here in Flatbush, an entire Japanese-style house was built as an advertising and marketing initiative. Though it had success in the press, the house was ultimately sold to Dr. Frederick Kohle in 1906 at below cost.

Today, however, it is certainly one of the most unique discoveries in the residential neighborhood. In 1997, the *New York Times* called it "perhaps New York's most unusual residence." There have been many myths surrounding the house over the years, including one claiming that it was built by the Japanese consul to the United States and that it was shipped piece by piece from Japan. None of the stories are true. The house was designed by John J. Petit of the firm Kirby, Petit & Green, notable for their work on Dreamland on Coney Island.

The current owners, Gloria and Albert Fischer, purchased the property in the 1970s. The Fischers have restored the house to its original green and orange paint scheme and eclectically decorated the interior with antiques collected over the course of over 40 years. The ground floor, apart from the kitchen, is in the same form it was in when the house was built. The stained glass windows, both on the exterior and within the house, still exist, along with the original woodwork. The Japanese influence can be felt through the structure of the interior, but less from the materials chosen. As such, the design preferences of the American elite at the time were melded with an outside influence. According to Andrew Dolkart, who wrote the Landmarks Preservation designation report for Prospect Park South, "The roof of the house seems to have originally been covered with Japanese-style tile."

Alvord is also responsible for the British-influenced street names in the neighborhood, renaming existing roads to Buckingham, Westminster, Albemarle and more.

ORIGINAL FURNITURE
OF THE BROOKLYN KINGS THEATRE

An immaculate restoration

1027 Flatbush Avenue
Brooklyn, NY 11226
www.kingstheatre.com
Transport: 2/5 to Beverly Road

The Brooklyn Kings Theatre, opened in 1929, was built as one of the five Loew's Wonder Theaters in the New York City area, the most opulent movie palaces in the country. The Loew's Kings Theatre was modeled after the Opera Garnier in Paris and the palace at Versailles. Flatbush was once one of the premier entertainment destinations in Brooklyn, and the revitalization of the neighborhood was one of the goals of the New York City Economic Development Corporation with a multi-year, $95 million renovation of the Kings Theatre.

Closed in 1977, the Kings Theatre had deteriorated extensively over the course of decades. Bats had taken up residence, and the ceiling and wall of the auditorium on stage left had collapsed.

The renovation was painstaking, with all the ornamentation hand painted from the ceiling to the end stands on each row of seats.

It can be hard to tell in the restoration what is original and what is not, a deliberate strategy. For example, the carpet, all 2,354 square feet of it, is a historical recreation. So are the tapestries, curtain and tassels. The chandeliers in the lobby are all original except for one, but on the mezzanine level, only one original remains.

As such, the furniture may be the most overlooked secret of the Brooklyn Kings Theatre. When the theater closed in 1977, the lobby furniture was given to one of its long-time managers, Dorothy Solomon Panzica, who brought the pieces to her summer home in Corning, New York. In 2013, at 100 years old, Panzica heard that the theater was going to be restored. She decided to donate the furniture back, whereupon the pieces underwent a $75,000 - $80,000 restoration.

Among the pieces include a console table made in Paris by André Lemoine, furniture maker to the court of Napoleon III. There are also Louis XVI-style chairs, ornate pieces worthy of a royal throne, and a lounge sofa. The management of the Kings Theatre made the decision to allow the furniture to be used, rather than roped off as if in a museum. You can find the pieces in the lobby, in the VIP room, and scattered throughout the theater.

A visit to the restored Brooklyn Kings Theatre, now used as a performing arts venue, is a must, but don't forget to pay attention to and sit on the historic furniture.

MONTHLY FREE TOUR OF THE WILD PARROTS OF BROOKLYN

Undisclosed location in Flatbush

www.brooklynparrots.com
Open the first Saturday of every month
Transport: 2/5 to Flatbush Av-Brooklyn College

The tale of the wild Brooklyn parrot, one of the most surprising finds in the borough, begins in Argentina. The bright green sub-tropical birds go by a few names – the Quaker Parrot, the Monk Parakeet or its Latin name *Myiopsitta monachus* – and have been in New York for over 40 years. Considered a pest to farmers in Argentina, the Quaker Parrot survived first an attempt at extermination.

In the 1970s, the Argentinian government launched a bounty program, compensating farmers for shooting the parrots. If the feet were sent to the agricultural bureau, the farmers would be paid a fixed rate for each parrot. This program became ripe for fraud, with farmers sending in the feet of chickens, pigeons and other birds. The program was shut down and the government pivoted its strategy. Instead of killing the birds, they would round them up and export them to countries like the United States, where exotic birds were being purchased as pets.

Meanwhile, in New York City, organized crime controlled the city's docks and airports. Shipments would routinely get intercepted by the Mafia and pilfered for some of their goods as kickback. One day, a container was opened at John F. Kennedy Airport and a flock of enterprising Quaker Parrots made their escape, flying both east to Long Island and west to Brooklyn and other parts of Queens. Other birds regularly escaped as a matter of course from broken shipping containers, pet stores, and private owners.

The transplanted parrots subsequently survived another eradication attempt by New York State in the late 1970s. But far from the pest they were once said to be, the parrot has actually proven to be a friendly neighbor. Stephen Baldwin, who runs the website *BrooklynParrots.com* says that some scientists believe the Quaker Parrots are an example of "charismatic megafauna," or species who survive due to their ability to charm humans. The parrots, which mate for life, are known for their intelligence and sociability – with a language system of at least 14 unique commands. At Green-Wood Cemetery in Brooklyn they have been welcomed and are considered a benefit, as their excrement does not damage the historic structures unlike other birds.

Baldwin estimates that there are about 150 Quaker Parrots in Brooklyn today. The location where you can see the parrots most up-close is on a leafy residential street in Flatbush. The birds relocated here after changes were made to the landscape at their previous residence at Brooklyn College (though you can still see some nests in the lights above the athletic field).

The best way to see the parrots is through a monthly free tour run by Baldwin. He does these "safaris" for awareness, hoping that the more people know about these parrots, the more they will see them as "part of the gorgeous mosaic of Brooklyn." To prevent poachers, who have come to capture the birds, he tells guests to keep the location secret. "I like to spread the word one by one," he says.

Neighbors have taken to the parrots and protect the birds by allowing for the creative nests to grow in street trees. Used to the four seasons, the Quaker Parrots stay in New York City all year round. Baldwin gives tours on the first Saturday of every month, alternating between Flatbush and Green-Wood Cemetery.

THE PUPPET LIBRARY

A lending library for giant puppets

Brooklyn College
Arts Lab at the Roosevelt House
Weekday afternoons, when Brooklyn College Community Partnership
afterschool program is open
Transport: 2/5 to Flatbush Av-Brooklyn College

I t seems that no matter where it goes, The Puppet Library always finds itself in a rather hidden spot. Until 2008, the museum was housed inside the Soldiers' and Sailors' Arch at Grand Army Plaza, a place the Puppet Museum librarian Theresa Linnihan says was "a mysterious place. People never knew you could go inside." There was a spiral staircase inside and

visitors could wander freely to take in the museum. Puppet shows would take place at the top of the arch interior. But when the arch started leaking and the roof fell in, the museum needed to find a new home – one big enough to house the collection.

The Puppet Library began in Boston, where it "sort of drifted into experience," says founder Sara Peattie, a puppeteer by training. Her partner George was living in New York City so the collection started to take hold there. When George died, Linnihan took over the library. She happened on the arch and fought to get the library in there.

Since 2008, the library has been located in a former gymnasium at the Roosevelt House at Brooklyn College, part of a space run by Brooklyn College Community Partnership, an after school program. The location has made the Puppet Museum even more obscure, and Linnihan says, "It's been more difficult to get the word out that the library is there." In fact, the Puppet Library does not have a website or a phone number.

But what is there is rather astounding and worth the trip. There are over 100 puppets, some as large as 20 feet tall, that sit on the bleachers of the gymnasium. These large-scale puppets have appeared in parades, in movies, even birthday parties. You can crawl into the puppets, or even take one out on a loan.

Nearby, in James Hall, is the Puppetry in Practice Center (PiP), a resource center founded in 1980. PiP started literally from a closet by Dr. Tova Ackerman, an adjunct professor at Brooklyn College then. The organization is now active in bringing visual and performing arts into public school classrooms to facilitate learning. "I felt that if the kids shared the characters and stories of different cultures, they'll be open to people of different kinds, and along the way they learn English," Tova says.

PiP programs help students develop a wide range of skills including cultural exploration, speaking and performance skills, and English language fluency through puppetry and the arts. The drop-in center is open 9am to 5pm, five days a week, and is used by teachers and students. The center is decorated with puppets from all around the world (that you can play with) and with a detailed model of the Brooklyn Bridge, used in one of PiP's classes. PiP's art director Xun Ye can be found here making incredibly detailed sculptures using flour dough. Lessons plans are also available online.

Puppetry in Practice is the reason why the Puppet Library was able to relocate to Brooklyn College. Dr. Ackerman found Linnihan a space large enough for her puppets at Brooklyn College when the space at Grand Army Plaza was no longer workable. Linnihan worked with PiP for about a year too, so although the two organizations are not formally connected, the puppet world is undeniably a close-knit one.

THE PACIFIER TREE

A neighborhood rite of passage

1450 48th Street
Brooklyn, NY 11218
Transport: D to 50th Street or F to Ditmas Avenue

On 48th Street, mid-block between 14th and 15th Avenues in Borough Park, is a six-floor apartment building called The Plymouth that dates from 1938. In front, a tree covered in pacifiers marks a rite of passage for the children and parents of this neighborhood. The tradition, which is said to have started here anywhere between the early 1980s and 2004, was initiated by a former superintendent of the building, Miro Dugandzic.

Spurred on by his wife, Dugandzic started hanging discarded pacifiers on the tree, which became a spot where parents would bring their children once they "graduated" from the pacifier stage. In 2012, it was reported that at least one new pacifier was added per week. They also fall off regularly from the weight of all the attachments, creating room for new additions.

Apartment resident Rachel Rhine told the *New York Times* in 2013, "I see mothers picking up their little kid and the kid actually puts it on and they say: 'O.K., say goodbye, no more. You're a big girl now.' It's kind of a celebration to say, 'That's where it goes and that's where it stays and that's the end of it.'"

48th Street, like many other streets in Hasidic Jewish neighborhoods, rings with the sound of children's voices. It's a reminder of a simpler past, kept alive in Borough Park and Williamsburg, when children were entrusted to play freely in their neighborhoods. Families are large in the Hasidic community, which means a plentiful supply of pacifiers. The 2010 Census found that Borough Park had the largest number of children under the age of one, twice that of the Upper West Side in Manhattan, which came in second.

The tradition of the pacifier tree has its origins in Scandinavia. The Danish island of Thuro has an elderberry tree where families have been leaving pacifiers for more than a half century at least, if not more. There are more such trees in Copenhagen and other cities throughout Denmark and Sweden, where the pacifiers are sometimes attached with notes. It's unclear whether there is any direct inspiration between the Brooklyn and European pacifier trees – most likely, they're united through common human experience.

TORAH ANIMAL WORLD

One of the most off-the-beaten path museums in NYC

1603 41st Street
Brooklyn, NY 11218
877-752-6286
Sunday–Thursday 9am–9pm by appointment only
Transport: F to Ditmas Avenue

The Hasidic Jewish neighborhoods in Brooklyn can be a mystery unto themselves, with the communities staunchly holding on to time-honored traditions. The architecture of the neighborhoods adhere to standardized patterns, as do the clothing of the community members and the social norms between them. But every so often, something stands out.

In the neighborhood of Borough Park, Rabbi Shaul Shimon Deutsch runs two museums side by side on the corner of 41st Street and 16th Avenue. The Living Torah Museum (see following double page) and Torah Animal World are two of the most off-the-beaten-path museums in New York City you can find. In fact, the Village Voice calls Torah Animal World "one of the weirdest and most glorious museums this weird and glorious city has ever seen."

Torah Animal World, filled with over $1.5 million in taxidermied animals, aims to have every animal and bird mentioned in the Torah on exhibit. All the animals died naturally in zoos or gaming reserves and are shown in "true-to-life" poses. Animals on display include lions, giraffes, a zebra, a black bear, a llama on skis, a penguin, bison, fish and much more.

There is also an exhibit of 24 birds from the Torah, many of which are displayed as if in flight. And lest we forget the smallest animals on the planet, there's an exhibit about the Shratzim, which includes insects and lizards, and another showcasing the animals in Perek Shirah (an ancient Jewish text), in a safari-like setting.

The aim of Torah Animal World goes beyond the bizarre. Deutsch started the museum as a way to visually teach children with dyslexia and learning disabilities about the Torah. He suffered from dyslexia himself as a child but can read numerous ancient languages. He thought that if children could touch things, they would be able to remember them differently. "We believe that if you can touch history, history will touch you," he says.

There is another location of Torah Animal World, located in the Catkills in Fallsburg, New York, that exhibits the animals of the Mishna and the Talmud.

LIVING TORAH MUSEUM

World's smallest Torah

1603 41st Street
Brooklyn, NY 11218
877-752-6286
Sunday–Thursday 9am–9pm by appointment only
Transport: F to Ditmas Avenue

Directly connected to Torah Animal World, the Living Torah Museum aims to further the study of the Torah through access to the items mentioned in the text, as well as pieces from the Biblical period in general: there's a Mesopotamian clay cuneiform tablet from

around 2037 B.C.E., a 3000-year-old wooden stylus, a 2300-year-old Greek soldier's helmet and sword, Egyptian headrests, a Persian King's scepter, and even an ancient Egyptian beer jug. Additional artifacts come from the era of the Mishna/Talmud, from about 200 to 500 C.E. Like Torah Animal World, everything here can be touched and worn.

The Living Torah Museum also has the distinction of holding the world's smallest Torah, created much more recently in about 2009. The scroll, made by Y. Chatzkelson Silversmiths, is only two inches tall and took several years to make. The rollers are made of sterling silver and the text is 1/32 of an inch high, painstakingly written in Jerusalem on vellum parchment with the help of a magnifying glass. The Torah comes in a silver ark and bima, with a magnifying glass included. It is certified by an Israeli verification expert and listed in the Guinness Book of World Records. It was originally commissioned by a man in upstate New York, who worked with different artisans to create the final product.

The Torah was sold in an auction for $150,000 and then donated to the Living Torah Museum. As a testament to the "living" part of the museum's name, the mini Torah is used every week for afternoon prayer during Shabbat, read by someone with 20/20 vision.

A bus that caters almost exclusively to Hasidic Jews

Servicing a route from Borough Park to Williamsburg, buses on the B110 route look much like municipal buses, although they are often wrapped in Hasidic advertising. The buses are also of a different shape than standard MTA buses, they do not take MetroCards, nor do they run on Friday nights or most of Saturday. The reason: they cater almost exclusively to Hasidic Jews. Since 1973, the B110 bus has been operated by the Private Transportation Corporation as a franchise with the New York City Department of Transportation. As such, by law, anyone can take it, but this does not happen in practice. At $3.25 a ride it costs more than an MTA fare. In 2011, following controversy about sex segregation on the bus – women were told verbally and through signage to sit in the back or take a women-only bus – there was the possibility that the city was going to shut the bus line down. Signs were made by the bus company to comply with anti-discrimination laws, but it appears that things have remained the same through de facto segregation. The bus route appears in signage on official city bus posts, but is not included on MTA bus maps.

ERUVIN

The enigmatic Jewish border marker

Eruvin enclose large areas; for a map of the Boro Park eruv (pictured), go to:
boroparkeruv.org

There's one way to get inside the mysteries of rule-bound Orthodox Jewish communities: explore the fringes. That's where you'll find an eruv, if you know where to look. The eruvin are unbroken lines of wire or nylon stretching overhead, usually from lamp posts. They completely enclose Orthodox territory – and non-Jewish territory – within a symbolic boundary.

According to Talmudic law, the home can be joined with a neighbor's home by a wall. The notion of "wall" can include one with doorways, one with big doorways, and even one composed of nothing but great yawning doorways framed by the slenderest supports – lamp posts, for example. Now make "neighbor" thousands of neighbors. This is an eruv: a vast collective household encircled by fishing line stretched across the urban landscape.

The lines are hard to find even when you know they're directly overhead. In the south of Boro Park, one of the largest Orthodox communities in the world, the Chinese, Russians, and Hispanics interviewed say they've never noticed the eruv. After a moment of wary courtesy ("Do you mind, can I ask why you are asking?") Joseph says the entire perimeter is checked before Sabbath. "The rabbi takes care of this thing," he says. "So I don't think about it."

There are over twenty eruvin in the city, including one in Manhattan that encloses the entire Upper West and East Sides from river to river.

VITAGRAPH STUDIOS SMOKESTACK AND TUNNEL

Where the film industry began

Intersection of East 15th Street and Locust Avenue
Midwood
Transport: Q to Avenue M

Vitagraph Studios was once the largest producer of motion pictures in the United States. In 2015, most of the major structures were demolished on the interior but local community and preservation groups are working to save the brick smokestack, with the word "VITAGRAPH" still visible on it. In addition, underground tunnels that connected the multiple buildings on the Vitagraph lot are still in existence.

The Vitagraph Company was founded in 1897 by J. Stuart Blackton, a former partner of Thomas Edison. The beginnings of the Vitagraph Company were scrappy, which enabled the company to use its profits to expand. Earlier buildings in the area were demolished as the company grew, but the oldest structures may have dated to 1908.

As the *Brooklyn Daily Eagle* reported in the 1920s, this four-acre studio was considered "one of the wonders of Brooklyn," and the "cradle of moving picture history," both a cutting-edge production facility and a "door to fame for many young Brooklyn movie actors and actresses." In the studio's heyday, the movie Peter Pan was shot here. Mary Pickford, Maurice Costello, and the Talmadge sisters filmed on the Vitagraph stages, and it is said that Leon Trotsky and Rudolph Valentino worked here as extras in the early parts of their careers. It's not an exaggeration to say that the Hollywood film industry had its start in Brooklyn. By 1912, the owners were making upwards of 5 million dollars a year.

The facility had a staff of 400 in 1920, and "vast laboratories, sunrooms, developing rooms, offices, and dressing rooms," wrote the *Brooklyn Daily Eagle*, "Eighty-seven miles of film a year were produced in the Brooklyn Plant." By 1925, Vitagraph had the largest motion picture library in the world. It even operated a theater in Times Square, having refurbished the Criterion Theater on 44th Street.

With the shift of the movie business to Los Angeles, the Vitagraph Company struggled. In 1925, it was purchased by Warner Brothers who waited four years before resuming production at the Brooklyn location for the new "talking pictures". It was thought that the proximity to Broadway and the Metropolitan Opera would make it more convenient for the recording of singing artists. Two new sound stages were built, with half a million dollars of upgrades to the studios.

But the revitalization was short lived. By 1931, Warner Brothers was only making short films in Brooklyn. Another revival attempt came in 1936 and yet another soundstage was built, but production was moved back to California in 1938. The facility continued to do film processing and was expanded again in the early 1950s to handle color production and 3D films. In 1953, NBC purchased the studio from Warner Brothers where it filmed soap operas such as "Another World" and other programs.

QUENTIN ROAD

Named for Theodore Roosevelt's son

From Stillwell Avenue to Kings HIghway
Transport: N to Kings Highway

South of Prospect Park, Brooklyn was laid out on a street grid system. East-west avenues were lettered A through Z, which intersected with numbered streets running north to south. A few of the lettered avenues were later bestowed new names, with Quentin Road the most famous.

In 1922, Avenue Q was rededicated Quentin Road in honor of Quentin Roosevelt, the youngest son of President Theodore Roosevelt.

Quentin died in World War I while serving as a lieutenant in France with the United States Army Air Service. At age four, his father became President of the United States, and he grew up rambunctiously in the White House. His crew of toddler friends played pranks on the Secret Service and were dubbed by Theodore Roosevelt the "White House Gang".

Quentin was shot down on July 14th, 1918 at the beginning of the Second Battle of the Marne. *The New York Times* reported that Quentin "stubbornly made repeated attacks" against seven German planes but was brought down near the town of Chambray. The Germans buried him with full military honors, saving his personal belongings (which included a pocket case), to send to his family. Nine years later, a flare gun with his name on it was found in a French battlefield.

In the *Boston Daily Globe*, Quentin's commanding captain wrote of his character as "easily the most popular man in his squadron," and noted his "square dealing and fairness." He also wrote of Quentin's bravery and recklessness. Quentin left formation on July 10th upon seeing German planes approaching from above and behind, taking the entire squadron on himself. He was shot down by Sergeant Thom of the Richtofen Circus, who had 24 confirmed kills at that point.

A memorial service, attended by high military officials and other notable personages took place at the Hotel St. George in Brooklyn Heights.

The first appearance of Quentin Road in the *Brooklyn Daily Eagle* was in 1922, but there was a suggestion to rename it as such as far back as 1910 by the residents of Manhattan Terrace, when Quentin Roosevelt was still growing up at the White House. The 1910 proposal to rename all of the lettered avenues was met with some disapproval for the use of English and foreign names.

The opposite effect

A letter from a Pennsylvania clergyman, whose brother had German prisoners under his command, showed that Quentin's death, though widely disseminated in Germany for propaganda purposes, had quite the opposite effect on the German populace. The fact that Quentin, the son of the American President, was killed fighting in one of the most dangerous areas of military activity made a sharp contrast with the sons of the Kaiser, who had "not yet been scratched."

THE BENSONHURST
STATUE HOUSE

A pop culture spectacle

2056 85th Street, Brooklyn, NY 11214
Private residence
Transport: D subway to 20 Avenue Station

In all of New York City there's nothing quite like the Bensonhurst Statue House. Located halfway down 85th Street between 20th and 21st Avenues, number 2056 would be fairly nondescript were it not for the nearly forty life-size sculptures of pop culture figures standing guard: Superman flies out from a second story balcony; Batman keeps watch at the foot of the driveway; Marilyn Monroe and Elvis flirt and croon; James Dean looks over at Humphrey Bogart; Betty Boop eyes an unseen interloper; and Dracula and Frankenstein look forebodingly from above the garage. The tableau is replete with kitschy accoutrements ranging from an old-school phone booth, street signs, a lamp post, and other mid-century memorabilia.

The whole creation is the work of Steve Campanella, a retired Marine who uses the spectacle to express his love of pop culture from his childhood and his deep pride in his hometown of Brooklyn; "Memory Lane" reads one sign attached to a lamp post. The driveway and garage are fashioned like the approach to the Brooklyn Battery Tunnel, with two "lanes" where you can choose Cash or E-ZPass. Many of the signs are about Brooklyn, including one that points to Ebbets Field (see page 86). Campanella calls it Steve's Playland and even more can be found inside his massive garage where thousands of collectors' items are stored.

The Bensonhurst Statue House is so renowned that former Brooklyn Borough President Marty Markowitz has paid a visit; he told the *New York Daily News*, "Steve is a real Brooklyn character." With a sense of humor and very self-aware of the oddity of his pastime, Campanella hung a sign on one of the sculptures that says "Pray for The Campanellas - especially Steve, who needs the most help."

THE NEW UTRECHT LIBERTY POLE

The last one in the thirteen original states

New Utrecht Reformed Church
18th Avenue and 84th Street, Brooklyn, NY 11214
718-236-0678
www.newutrechtchurch.org
www.historicnewutrecht.org
Transport: D train/18th Av

The Liberty Pole in Manhattan plays a key role in the earliest days of the Revolution, but the one that rises high in front the New Utrecht Reformed Church can lay greater claim to authenticity. The Manhattan pole references the one that made history; the one in New Utrecht is living history. The sixth in an unbroken series at the same site that goes back to 1783, the pole is the last remaining in the thirteen original states.

The current monument, a metal mast 106 feet high, was recycled from the 1939-40 World's Fair, and looks like it will last for a while. Previous poles were more perishable; their history is spelled out in a series of plaques, streaked in verdigris. The first was erected when the British finally left New York after an occupation that lasted the duration of the war; townsfolk fired cannons and made "other demonstrations of joy." It was the first time the American flag flew over New Utrecht. Successive poles followed in 1834, 1867, 1910 (struck by lightning), 1936, and the one you see today in 1946.

"It's my understanding," says David Elligers, "that the metal weathervane is original." Elligers, a tall, older man with glasses, is the president of Friends of New Utrecht. He has a steady manner and a universal knowledge of the area's history: when he says it's his "understanding," it's as much as a statement of fact. He has come to direct a tour of the New Utrecht Cemetery for "Liberty Weekend," an event that takes place on the first weekend of June to celebrate the pole, the church, and America's independence. Recordings of marching band music play over speakers as a couple of soldiers in flawless kit – right down to the breeches and antique round-rimmed eyewear – lean on their muskets. "I belong to the 23rd Regiment of Foot Royal Welsh Fusiliers," announces the Redcoat, whose face is sweating under a thick bearskin hat. The Bluecoat belongs to the New York Second Regiment and sips from a functioning canteen. Behind them loiter several men in Civil War uniforms, as though the time portal stood open a little too long. Now and then strolling Chinese or Hispanic families – the bulk of this neighborhood's demographic today – pause to try and figure out what these characters in front of the church are up to. Then they pass on.

ORIGINAL TOWN LAYOUT OF GRAVESEND

The first woman to settle a village in the New World

27 Gravesend Neck Road
Brooklyn, NY 11223
Transport: F to Avenue U

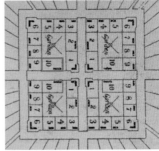

Gravesend Neck Road, often referred to as Neck Road (like the subway station), is a road that dates to the colonial era. Along this road is the Van Sicklen House, popularly known as Lady Moody's house, considered one of the oldest surviving Dutch American homes in the United States. Though not the oldest house in New York City (that distinction goes to the Pieter Claesen Wyckoff House, also in Brooklyn), portions of the Van Sicklen house date to the early 18th century. Though the Van Sicklen House is not the house of Lady Deborah Moody herself, it sits on the part of a lot where her original home stood at 27 Gravesend Neck Road.

Lady Moody was a particularly notable New Yorker. In 1645, she was the first woman to receive a land charter in the colonies and subsequently founded the town of Gravesend.

But even before this, Lady Moody was making waves in England. She had been married to Sir Henry Moody, but was widowed in 1629. Her out-of-the-box religious beliefs got her banned from London, upon which she relocated to the New World. She was also pushed out of Saugus, Massachusetts for not conforming to Puritan practices (she did not believe in the baptism of infants), but found welcome reception in Dutch New Amsterdam, bringing with her a group of fellow religious dissenters.

The town plan for Gravesend was, if not the first, one of the earliest planned communities in the United States. There were four quadrants within a 16-acre plot of land, each with 10 houses surrounding a central common square. Farmland began beyond the four quadrants. Although most of the earliest settlements have been demolished and their street plans lost, the original plan of Gravesend amazingly still exists in the street grid today.

If you start at the west end of Gravesend Neck Road, you'll find that the four quadrangles are still there, angled against the rest of the Brooklyn street grid. The quadrangle is bordered by Village Road North, Village Road South, Village Road East and Van Sicklen Street, with MacDonald Avenue and Gravesend Neck Road bisecting it.

The common square in the southwest quadrant was used as the Gravesend Cemetery, which still exists today.

Lady Moody's House, landmarked in 2016, is located in the northeast quadrangle across from the northern entrance of the cemetery. In the southeast quadrant, Village Court, a dead end road, juts into the former common square. Today, houses line this road.

ABANDONED YELLOW SUBMARINE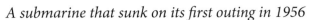

A submarine that sunk on its first outing in 1956

Calvert Vaux Park Greenway
Coney Island Creek
Transport: D to Bay 50th Street

Coney Island Creek is home to a small boat graveyard, within which sits a curious submarine. The 45 foot steel submarine is the handiwork of local ship builder Jerry Bianco. It was named the Quester I, but is affectionately known as the "Yellow Submarine," a reference to its bright yellow tower that has rusted with time.

Bianco hoped to use the Quester I to locate and raise the Andrea Doria, an Italian ocean liner that sank after colliding with the MS Stockholm on its maiden voyage in 1956 en route from New York City. Of the 1,134 passengers on board, 46 lost their lives. Like the Titanic before it, the Andrea Doria was touted as the safest ship ever built, a marvel of the latest technology.

Like the Andrea Doria, the Quester I also sank on its first outing. There wasn't enough ballast in the ship to keep it upright and it got stuck in the mud of Coney Island Creek. There were not enough funds to raise it and the Quester I has been in Coney Island Creek ever since.

The submarine has become such a landmark of the area that the New York City Parks Department installed a sign about it on a traffic railing on Coney Island in view of the sunken boat.

Coney Island Creek is a tidal estuary that once separated Coney Island from the mainland of Brooklyn. The creek was originally far shorter, ending where the Cropsey Avenue bridge is today. It was extended as a canal all the way to Sheepshead Bay in the 1700s as an initiative of Thomas Stilwell, who once owned all of Coney Island. It has since been filled back in.

Coney Island Creek history is also filled with somewhat morose details. This is where the landscape designer Calvert Vaux, most famous for designing Central Park and Prospect Park with Frederick Law Olmstead, died. It was never determined whether it was a suicide or an accident in the fog.

In more recent times, the creek has been blamed for much of the devastating floods on Coney Island and in Gravesend during Hurricane Sandy. It is also the location of one of the city's Combined Sewer Outflows. In heavy rains when the stormwater system is overloaded, a combination of raw sewage and rainwater is released into the creek. Nonetheless, this has not stopped people from actively fishing in the creek.

POLAR BEAR PLUNGE

Looking the coming year in the face

Coney Island Boardwalk
Annually, January 1
The Polar Bear Club swims throughout the winter; check website:
www.polarbearclub.org
Transport: D, F, N and Q trains/Coney Island – Stillwell Av

Jumping into the Atlantic Ocean in the middle of winter sounds like a bad idea. And it is. It's a supremely bad idea. This is why people come to take part in the Polar Bear Plunge, held at Coney Island every year. If it were especially smart or easy, there would be no point.

"It's like looking the coming year in the face and saying: I got you," says one of a group of shivering men from Maspeth, Queens, waiting on the boardwalk before the mad rush down the beach and into the freezing ocean. "It's mainly for the fun," says another. They are interrupted by what you may assume is their chief: a swaggering bear of a man who sports a terrycloth robe, a dozen Mardi Gras-style beaded necklaces, a stocking cap, and a bushy beard flecked with snot. "Look," he says with a beer-scented growl. "Look. If we don't have a heart attack, we get to live another year. If we drop dead, our problems are over. Happy New Year."

Togetherness is the theme of the event, and many attendees come in teams: groups united by costumes or neighborhood. The crowd is, it seems, entirely New York City; insane bravado is not on the tourist agenda. Many are repeat swimmers. "You do it the first year and you think: that was amazing," says Matthew from Brooklyn. "And every year on the train ride down you think: why am I doing this again? It's freezing. But confronting this with a bunch of people makes it better."

The event is sponsored, and it may be one undertaking where the level of control and organization goes totally unresented, although you're as likely to find anxiety as reassurance in the collection of ambulances that flank the boardwalk entrance, and the small Coast Guard fleet out on the dead grey ocean. And in fact, the experiences leading up to the heart-stopping plunge are the real torment: it's already so cold out in the air, as soon as you've dived in the water, your frail body seems beyond caring. Screaming seems to help (there's a lot of screaming).

"It's an exhilly, unh-exhilarating experience!" says dripping John Esposito, a Coney Island native. "It's great going in, great feeling it. One of the top New York traditions. Par-puh-party of the year, that's it."

TOPSY MEMORIAL

Electrocuting an elephant

Coney Island Museum
1208 Surf Avenue, Brooklyn
www.coneyisland.com/museum.shtml
Thursday-Sunday 12pm-6pm
Transport: D, Q, N and F trains/Coney Island – Stillwell Av

I t's saying much that a peepshow memorial to an electrocuted elephant is not exactly out of place on Coney Island. "The Playground of the World" has bright lights and roller coasters and mermaids, but there is something dark about the place, something one-eyed and out of tune, a shadow beckoning from the back flap of a circus tent. It's what artist Lee Deigaard calls "the underbelly to the glitz," and her *Topsy Memorial* in the Coney Island Museum sums it up.

The memorial is in the form of an old-fashioned mutoscope, a crank-driven contraption invented in the late 1800s that works like a flip-book: a stack of images printed on cards cascade on a wheel to create a small, and silent, and weirdly private little film experience. The subject is one of the strangest episodes in New York history. On January 4, 1903, Topsy, a 30-year-old circus elephant, was executed by electricity at Coney Island's Luna Park. Her crime was attacking her brutish handlers, who prodded her with pitchforks and reportedly fed her lighted cigarettes. The man in charge of the electrocution was none other than Thomas Edison.

Edison came to elephant disposal through a public feud about the distribution of electricity; the inventor had patents on direct current (DC), while his rival George Westinghouse pushed alternating current (AC). Unable to attack AC's distinct distribution advantages, mean-spirited Edison played another angle: that AC was dangerous. He "Westinghoused" dogs and cats and livestock to death, and when he learned that Luna Park wanted to put an elephant down, he sensed a commercial spectacle. A crowd of 1,500 gathered to watch the execution, which Edison also filmed and distributed throughout the United States.

"What happened to her should remain a touchstone," says Deigaard in a phrase you don't hear every day, "for empathy at large as well as for elephants." Her memorial mutoscope in the Coney Island Museum has a jar of pennies next to it. Put one in, press your face to the viewing port, and turn the crank. The title flickers: "ELECTROCUTING AN ELEPHANT – Thomas A. Edison." Keep cranking and keep watching, with a voyeur's vague guilt, as Topsy, wearing copper electrodes on her feet, is led into frame.

ABRAHAM LINCOLN HORSE
AT THE B&B CAROUSELL

A special horse in a historic carousel

Steeplechase Plaza
Coney Island Boardwalk West
Brooklyn, NY 11224
www.lunaparknyc.com
Hours vary, check calendar
Transport: D/N/F/Q to Coney Island - Stillwell Avenue

In 2013, the B&B Carousell made a triumphant return to the Coney Island Boardwalk. It is the last of the approximately 25 hand-carved carousels that once dotted Coney Island in its heyday.

Born and bred on Coney Island, the carousel dates to 1906 – its frame at least. Most of the horses, designed by carousel designer Charles Carmel, date from 1926.

Carmel was known to adorn his horses with many trimmings, such as tassels, flowers, decorative blankets, jewels and more. The carousel itself is named after Bishoff & Brienstein, who were responsible for bringing the ride back to Coney Island in 1935, after a stint in New Jersey.

Its unique spelling (with a double 'L') dates back to its creation.

Like much of Coney Island in the latter half of the 20th century, the carousel had fallen into decline and disrepair. In 2005, the City of New York purchased the amusement to save it from the chopping block. A meticulous multi-year restoration began in 2008 in Marion, Ohio, under the supervision of Todd W. Goings, one of the last experts in carousel restoration.

Goings only uses techniques that the original builders employed, particularly appropriate for the B&B Carousell, which was built by craftsmen in the once-thriving carousel industry on Coney Island. In addition to removing twenty layers of thick paint from the horses, Goings repaired the 50 wooden animals using only dowels and glue.

Every carousel has a lead horse, but the one on the B&B Carousell is particularly distinguished from the rest: older than the others, it is the only one that was not designed by Charles Carmel. In the restoration process, Goings discovered the signature of another Coney Island carver of much renown, Marcus Charles Illions. The horse, with a relief of American President Abraham Lincoln on its side, is one horse of four that were created by Illions in 1909 to commemorate the birth of Lincoln. It is the only one that is still displayed in public – multi-colored rhinestones, cloak of armor and all.

Today, the B&B Carousell is operated by the new Luna Park. It sits on Steeplechase Plaza, near the entrance to the former Luna Park. It has a new climate controlled glass pavilion for all-weather operation. Goings also refurbished the German-made 66-key band Gebruder Bruder organ, which once again serenades riders and those walking by on the boardwalk. In early 2016, the carousel was added to the National Register of Historic Places. More than a restored piece of history, the carousel represents where America's Playground is evolving. As Seth Pinksy, former president of the New York City Economic Development Corporation stated at the 2013 unveiling, "There are very few surviving carousels of this vintage. It's historic and it's brand new, and that's what Coney Island is."

GRANDMOTHER'S PREDICTIONS FORTUNE TELLING MACHINE

One of the world's oldest arcade machines

Inside Deno's Wonder Wheel Amusement Park
3059 Denos Vourderis Place
Brooklyn, NY 11224
www.wonderwheel.com
Hours vary, check calendar
Transport: D/N/F/Q to Coney Island - Stillwell Avenue

Fortune telling machines are part of the history of amusement parks in the 20th century, and one of the grande dames is Grandmother's Predictions, located inside Deno's Wonder Wheel Amusement Park. Akin to other proper ladies, her exact age is rather vague, but she appears to have been built around 1929. According to Justin Rivers, writer and guide who leads the Secrets of Coney Island Tour for the New York City-based publication *Untapped Cities*, the automaton was purchased by the Ward family, one of Coney Island's great financiers, who owned the Wonder Wheel and many other amusements.

Dennis D. Vourderis, who currently owns the amusement park with his brother Steve, tells us that Grandma came to the Wonder Wheel "in the 1930s and has remained in the same exact location since" (apart from a restoration after Superstorm Sandy). The Vouderis family has been offered large sums for Grandma, as it's a prized collector's item, but Dennis says they have "refused as we had promised to never separate her from the wheel. My family was under strict orders to *never* let Grandma leave the Wonder Wheel site as she was the guardian of the wheel."

Put in fifty cents and the mannequin Grandma will start turning her head from side to side and start breathing. Her hand will move over the playing cards in front of her, the candle will light up, her eyes will open and a fortune will emerge from the slot. Printed on the slip of paper will be not only a prophecy, but also lucky numbers and astrological information. Those familiar with the 1988 Tom Hanks movie *Big* will recognize Zoltar, another fortune telling machine located just next to Grandma.

Grandmother's Predictions survived extensive damage from Superstorm Sandy in 2012 and was lovingly brought back to life in the specialty carnival workshop of Bob Yorburg in Westchester, New York. During the multi-month restoration, Grandma received a replacement set of vintage wax hands, a new wig and a new dress. Then, using a twin game, Yorbug also reconstructed the interior mechanism.

Yorburg told the *Wall Street Journal* in 2012 that "this stuff was made to last forever, and it really can. It's actually mechanical, so it's not like this is shorting out like a modern arcade game." Inside, he saw how Grandma had been repaired over the years – with paper clips and glue. He even found a vintage bottle of Clorox bleach from the 1920s and a mid-century bathroom light inside the machine.

The wooden cabinet that protects Grandma now was added as part of the 2013 restoration. Vintage photographs of Coney Island from the 1970s show a red metal case instead. The price has also risen from 10 cents to 25 cents to the current 50 cents.

GRASHORN BUILDING

The oldest building on Coney Island

1104 Surf Avenue
Brooklyn, NY 11224
Transport: D/N/F/Q to Coney Island - Stillwell Avenue

I t looks like an abandoned building today, but at the corner of Surf Avenue and Jones Walk, a boarded up wooden clapboard house is all that remains of the oldest building on Coney Island. Built sometime in the early to mid-1880s by Henry Grashorn, the Grashorn Building is a Victorian style building with a mansard roof that was allegedly built originally as a hotel. Grashorn quickly transformed it into a hardware store around 1898: the shop furnished the nuts and bolts for the major amusement parks on Coney Island – Luna Park, Steeplechase and Dreamland. There was once a porch that wrapped around the building, under which household wares and candy were sold.

Henry Grashorn was a prominent Coney Island resident, serving as the Trustee to the Coney Island Hospital, director of the Coney Island Bank and founder and President of the Coney Island Mardi-Gras Association, of which the famous Coney Island Mermaid Parade "is a direct descendant," contends *The New York Times*.

Today, the Grashorn Building, like many other properties along Surf Avenue, is owned by Thor Equities. The detailed metal trimming at the top of the roof is now lost, along with the chimneys, but it is possible that other original details and the dormer windows still exist under the current synthetic siding that covers the original façade.

Until 2009, the bottom floor housed skeeball games and other amusements, similar to those on the rest of Jones Walk. The tenant told the website *Amusing the Zillion* that rent had tripled to $24,000 and he could not renew. Since then, the building has only been rented for a smattering of short-term uses, including a film location for the HBO Series *Vinyl* (produced by Martin Scorcese, Mick Jagger and Terence Winter), for the show *Bored to Death*, and as an office for the production team of *Men in Black III*.

Fearing demolition, preservation organizations such as The Municipal Art Society and the New York Landmarks Conservancy have been advocating to landmark the Grashorn Building since at least 2009 without success. For now, it's still listed for lease by Thor Equities.

CONEY ISLAND SIDESHOW SCHOOL

*Learn how to breathe fire, swallow swords, hammer
a nail into your skull, charm a snake and more*

Coney Island USA Museum
1208 Surf Avenue
Brooklyn, NY 11224
718-372-5159
info@coneyisland.com
www.coneyisland.com
Sideshow performance schedule on website
Transport: D/N/F/Q to Coney Island - Stillwell Avenue

For those who fear that Coney Island may be losing its freaky side, look no further than the Sideshow School. Here you can learn how to breathe fire, swallow swords, hammer a nail into your skull, charm a snake and more. The 3-day class costs $1000, a pricey sum for those simply curious, but many who attend are magicians and circus performers honing their trade. They come from all around the country, as this is the only school of its kind in the United States keeping the sideshow tradition alive.

While you lie on a bed of nails, you may have someone sledgehammer a cinder block in two on top of you. You'll learn how to walk on broken glass and rub your face with the shards, maybe even do a handstand on top of it. It's a "safe controlled environment to learn some of the most dangerous things," says Adam Rinn, one of the professors at the Sideshow School. Rinn shows that the secrets of the trade are all related to biology and physics, and here they learn the safest and simplest ways to perform these tricks. Still, you'll have to sign a waiver and don't expect to leave without losing a little blood.

The Sideshow School is part of the Coney Island USA Museum, located in the landmarked Childs Restaurant building on Surf Avenue. The building has served as a restaurant and casino in the past, as well as the site of David Rosen's Wonderland Circus Sideshow, which began in the 1950s. The Coney Island Museum relocated here in 2007, but has been running the Sideshow School since 2002.

Even if you don't want to put yourself through the Sideshow School, you can catch the sideshow performances and see feats performed by notable professionals in the field. It's the last traditional 10-in-1 continuous sideshow performance in an amusement context, the type once popular not only in the circus but also in vaudeville and burlesque shows. The sideshow performance here is scripted with historical dialogue, so you'll be getting the true old-school experience.

It's hard not to wonder how past and present will play out in the contested space that is Coney Island today, but as long as the Coney Island USA Museum is here, the sideshow is here to stay. "You know, no matter what happens around us, whether it's development or destruction," Rinn asserts, "We will be here holding that torch, carrying the flame, and saying yes, you know, it is good to be a freak."

Classes are limited to ten students at a time and you must be aged 18 or older to participate.

SHEEPSHEAD BAY BUNGALOWS

An old world community

Greenlawn Bungalow Community
Emmons Avenue
Transport: B/Q to Sheepshead Bay

If you know where to look, there are many old world spots in New York City. One particularly quaint find is the bungalow community in Sheepshead Bay. Starting in the mid-1800s, southern Brooklyn became a popular summer resort and tourist destination locale. Hotels, new roads, and new housing joined the fishing cottages on Sheepshead Bay. The arrival of the Sheepshead Bay Race Track and the Coney Island Jockey Club brought the area further renown. In 1911, the first successful cross-country airplane flight took off from the racetrack. The aviation daredevil Calbraith Perry Rodgers piloted the Wright Brothers plane (named the Vin Fiz after sponsor J. Ogden Armour's grape soft drink) to the Pacific Ocean, crashing 16 times en route.

In the 1920s, developer Robert Densely filled the waterfront marshland with sand from Sheepshead Bay and built a community of bungalows. Densely laid out the street plan and named many of the roads after his friends and associates. The one-story wooden cottages are accessible via pedestrian courts and alleys, beautified with landscaped walkways. Many of them have small gardens. Though nearly a century has passed, the bungalow community is still little known, even to New Yorkers. One owner of numerous properties in the Greenlawn Bungalow Community told photographer Nathan Kensinger in 2015, "It's a very unique, close-knit community, and a lot of people don't even know it is there. They have no idea. And if they ever walked in and saw it, they'd be like 'Oh my god, look at this – this is in Brooklyn?'"

But the low-lying nature of these communities, makes these bungalows susceptible to flooding and storms. Hurricane Sandy hit the area hard, destroying some homes outright. The New York Rising Community Reconstruction Program noted that 220 homes along Emmons Avenue were up to five feet below street level and not connected to city drainage infrastructure.

Many homes, requiring extensive rehabilitation, were sold. By 2015, the Complete Streets rehabilitation of Emmons Avenue was underway, with the installation of stormwater and streetscape improvements. The inner courts were being evaluated for resiliency improvements.

Despite those willing to stay, there are plans to demolish and rebuild some of the bungalows, and to raise the homes. In addition, larger scale buildings are going up around these cottages, the fruits of a neighborhood upzoning. All this means you should definitely visit soon, before more changes take place in this seaside neighborhood.

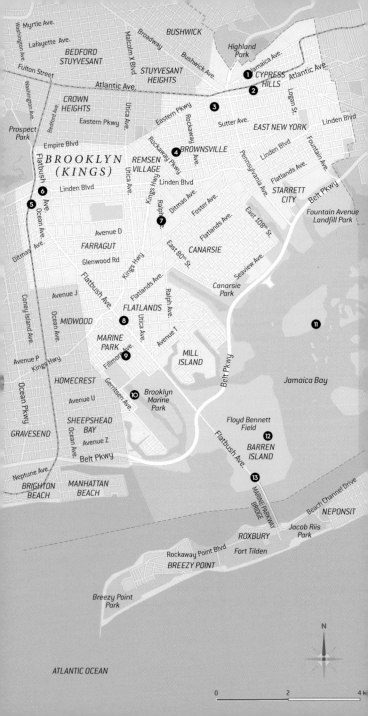

East to the borough border

RIDGEWOOD RESERVOIR

Where Brooklyn once got its water

Enter through Highland Park
Tours of Ridgewood Reservoir are given by the non-profit organization NYC H20
Transport: J/Z to Van Siclen Avenue

In 1858, a reservoir was built to serve the growing city of Brooklyn, still an independent jurisdiction from the city of New York. Like Manhattan, Brooklyn originally supplied water to its residents through private wells and pumps, and later through privately run companies. The Ridge-

wood Reservoir was the first large-scale attempt by the city to not only systematically provide for current demand, but also to plan for the future growth of the city.

Work on the Ridgewood Reservoir site began in 1856. By 1858, water was entering the two first basins. It was originally planned that the reservoir would have a capacity of 154 million gallons and would be filled with water sourced from collecting ponds in Queens and Long Island.

The water was brought in through a masonry conduit, which follows the path of what is Conduit Avenue today, and was controlled through a system of gatehouses and pumping stations. The engineering feat was so exciting that 30,000 people attended the opening ceremony of the Ridgewood Reservoir in 1859.

To satisfy increasing demand, a third basin was added later. As the decades passed, water closer to the city became more polluted and Brooklyn searched for sources further and further east. Water was even being tapped from Long Island aquifers but problems were about to come to a head.

Silt and salt water intrusion in Long Island water created difficulties for the reservoir system. Plus, Suffolk County passed laws banning Brooklyn from taking any of its water. Soon, it became clear that the Croton Aqueduct system (see from the same publisher the guide *Secret New York – An Unusual Guide*), which moved water by gravity from the Catskills to Manhattan, would be more cost effective and of better quality. Water thus became a key factor in the consolidation of Brooklyn into the City of New York in 1898.

For those of a more active bent, the remnants of the Ridgewood Reservoir experiment can still be seen within Highland Park, land on the border of Queens that Brooklyn purchased in 1891 to protect its water system. A few years ago, walking paths were installed around the basins, two of which have been drained. Along this walk, you will discover the brick foundations that supported the walls of the reservoir and a former gatehouse. One reservoir still contains fresh water (though at a lower level than the original reservoir) and has become a habitat for migrating birds.

Force Tube Avenue

Nearby, you can also find the abandoned force tubes that once pumped water from various collections points up into the reservoir. The three foot by four foot tunnel could pump 14 million gallons a day and persists under the very functionally named road "Force Tube Avenue," which cuts diagonally southeast from the Highland Park through the street grid to Fulton Street.

EMPIRE STATE DAIRY TILE MURALS ②

*Likely the largest murals by the American Encaustic
Tiling Company still existing*

2840 Atlantic Avenue
Brooklyn, NY 11207
Transport: J/Z to Van Siclen Avenue

Built in 1914 when the company was known as Borden's Dairy Factory, the complex of Empire State Dairy includes five buildings within a 76,375 square foot property. Of particular importance is the presence of two vertical tile murals on the façade, a site-specific commission for the Empire State Dairy building, produced under the oversight of Leon Solon, the art director of the American Encaustic Tiling Company. The Ohio-based firm was once the largest tile producer in the world, with a showroom in midtown Manhattan. The company did experimental work for the first New York City subway line, and although it did not win the final bid (which went to Carrere and Hastings), some test tiles remain at the Columbus Circle station, revealed and shown to the public following a 2007 renovation.

According to Michael Padwee, a historian and tile collector fighting to save Empire State Dairy since the 1990s, the two tile murals on the façade of the building are "probably the largest murals by this company that are still existing." They show a pastoral scene of cows alongside dairy workers wearing traditional German clothing. Padwee believes these tiles were made using the wet process, rather than any mass-production method. The bright glazed tiles are in high relief, a style known as majolica. This pottery style debuted in Europe and was popularized at the Great Exhibition in 1851, held at London's Crystal Palace.

The buildings have not been used as a dairy factory since the 1950s, and a neighborhood rezoning plan in 2016 had put many un-landmarked buildings in East New York at risk, although then-Landmarks Preservation Commission chair Meenakshi Srinivasan acknowledged at the time, "The Empire State Dairy buildings are some of the most impressive and historically significant in East New York." In December 2017 the building was officially designated a New York City landmark.

During the American Revolutionary War, British and hired Hessian soldiers marched overnight on the Jamaica Pass, in the area now known as East New York, to surprise George Washington's troops in the Battle of Brooklyn in 1776. Following this illustrious history, East New York was settled and incorporated into New York City in fits and starts, perhaps never quite fulfilling the dream of the original speculative landowner, John Pitkin, who wanted to create a rival city to New York here.

For more than fifty years, East New York remained a somewhat forgotten transportation junction, struggling through social and economic issues prompted by decades of neglect and questionable urban policy. In recent years, renewed interest in East New York was generated by city government, interested in rezoning the neighborhood to encourage economic growth, long-term development and affordable housing inventory.

BROOKLYN VINYL WORKS

One of only two vinyl making facilities in New York City

129 Powell Street
Brooklyn, NY 11212
718-485-4606
info@brooklynvinylworks.com
www.brooklynvinylworks.com
By appointment

Inside a non-descript two-floor industrial building in Brownsville, a humming production facility making vinyl records uses the same methods forged more than half a century ago. Brooklyn Vinyl Works, founded by Will Socolov, is one of only two vinyl making facilities in New York City. Socolov has extensive experience both in the production of vinyl records and on the recording side. He was the co-founder of Sleeping Bag Records and Freeze Records, one of the earliest distributors of Jay-Z's music.

Between 2013 and 2014, vinyl sales doubled in the United States. Recording artists today can wait up to six months to get their music onto vinyl, due to a growing demand for the output. Vinyl is known to have a warmer, more dynamic sound, and even young music enthusiasts are part of this movement back to records.

Socolov starting pressing records in a facility in Manhattan and in 2003 officially opened up EKS Manufacturing, located in Brooklyn, which made over 8 million records in a decade. Rising rents led to its closure in 2013, but Socolov quickly looked for a way to keep going. Raising money from investors and putting in his own funds, he adapted this building in Brownsville almost from scratch, even bringing in electricity and gas. And despite a failed Kickstarter campaign in 2015, Socolov decided to "open the factory no matter what."

Brooklyn Vinyl Works operates on the four record presses Socolov already owned; his team has decades of experience not only making records, but also repairing antiquated, out-of service equipment. Business has been strong and he aims to have the factory running 24 hours a day, which he says is also better for the equipment.

The factory presses 12" vinyl in a variety of colors, with an approximately eight to ten week turnaround. It's a full-service firm, so they master, plate, label, make jackets and inserts, and even shrink-wrap the records. The next step for Sokolov is to get more presses and newer equipment. "I don't know if it's gonna be the gold mine that everybody sort of says it is, but it is very popular," Socolov told the publication *Untapped Cities*, "I believe that this business is going to have a long life."

HEADQUARTERS OF MURDER, INC.

"Do you want to wind up in a landfill somewhere, stabbed with an ice pick?"

75 Livonia Avenue
Brooklyn, NY 11212

Unbeknownst to most customers of a mundane bodega in Brownsville, 75 Livonia Street was once the headquarters of Murder, Inc., a savage Mafia death squad created by the National Crime Syndicate. Active in the 1930s and 1940s, Murder Inc. was staffed by Italian American and Jewish gangsters from Brownsville, Ocean Hill and East New

centuries. This creek was also an original port of entry for the Dutch and an important trading dock for south Brooklyn. In the mid-1600s, Hugh Gerritsen built a grist mill upon this creek. According to the New York City Department of Parks and Recreation it was the first tide-powered mill in North America.

The mill ground flour, corn and grains for the troops in General George Washington's army in the American Revolutionary War when they were stationed in Brooklyn.

It was later captured and used by Hessian soldiers, contracted military from present-day Germany who fought for the British. You can find an old advertisement in the *Brooklyn Daily Eagle* from January 1849, noting "a complete and thorough repair," to the mill and offering "All kinds of Grain ground and attended to with dispatch." The Gerritsen grist mill operated until 1889.

The Gerritsen family property was sold in 1899 to Gilded Age tycoon William C. Whitney, who built a country estate where he could train his racehorses. He donated the property to the city before his death in 1904, and in 1928, the Whitney estate announced that they would restore the mill.

Historian Tom Whitford has called the mill, "an absolute marvel" and quite advanced technologically, able to operate continuously even with the ocean tides. Whitford says the mill was also used as a place for social gathering (ice skating in winter on the mill pond, picnics in summer) and a place for harvesting oysters. It was even used as a place for auctions, as seen in an 1864 newspaper announcement.

By 1930, the *Brooklyn Daily Eagle* was noting that "hoodlums and vandals [had] done considerable damage to the Whitney mill and dam property." In 1931, the community was expressing concern for its "neglected condition." The *Brooklyn Daily Eagle* reported that only one side of the house was intact, with an observer saying the other sides were "looking like the battle front in France." "Haste is vital in Restoring of Gerritsen Mill," the headline proclaimed. By 1932, some work was underway to repair the walls and foundations. Additional funds were appropriated in 1934 for a full restoration.

But in 1935, after exterior renovation was completed, the house was burned down, possibly by an arsonist. In low tide however, you can still see the remnants of the dam and the foundations of the mill. You can also see the pilings from a bulkhead built as part of a grand park and athletic facility planned for Marine Park. The never-realized design by Charles Downing Lay even won the silver medal at the 1939 Olympics in Berlin when the event had an architectural competition.

To get to this spot, start at the Salt Marsh Nature Center and take the nature trail that runs parallel to Burnett Street. The pilings from the mill can only be seen at very low tide.

KAYAK IN JAMAICA BAY

Out among forbidden isles

Parks Department offers free instruction and kayaks
For more freedom, Wheel Fun Rentals keeps kayaks at Riis Landing and Canarsie
www.wheelfunrentals.com/ Locations/New-York-2

The islands of Jamaica Bay are mysterious clumps of emerald marshland lying low out on the water. One of them, Broad Channel, harbors the Jamaica Bay Wildlife Refuge, which is the country's largest such refuge fully within city limits: 330 species of birds have been spotted there, or about half of all the species in the Northeast. The other islands are strictly forbidden. In 2007, New York magazine floated a reporter on a Crusoe-style survival mission to the largest of them: he sent out an SOS by text after one day. If you think you might do better, and know how to leave birds alone, enjoy. The way to get out is by kayak.

Voyaging under your own power, especially in a stealthy craft that connotes the Noble Savage, is good for a pretty visceral thrill of independence. Jamaica Bay is in the lee of the Rockaway peninsula of Queens so the water, except when combed out in the wakes of passing boats, is calm. There are dozens of islands, and while you're not supposed to set foot on them, many are squiggled with channels that you can explore. The shores of the larger ones are dotted with the wrecks of boats, as though a modest apocalypse has just occurred, but the low grassy islets are wonderfully wild, untouched, rimmed in mussels and thriving with birds. "You'll see the whole array," says Parks ranger John Daskalakis. "Gulls, geese, sandpipers, plovers. They give you this look like: *What are you doing in my place?*"

The most curious part about being out among the lonely marsh grass, listening to the cackle of seabirds, is looking beyond at a distant skyline that is as urban as it gets. Your phone still works. You can set the oar athwart the kayak, call your sister and describe the scene, then take a pic and send it to her, then check the map for the little blue dot of your present location: afloat in a channel twisting through a desert isle. Then slip overboard for a swim before paddling back.

Mau Mau Island, a manmade island

Start at the Marine Park Salt Marsh Nature Center
The best way to see Mau Mau Island is by kayak or canoe on trips run by
the New York City Parks Department. You can also see it on a nature trail
that starts at the Marine Park Salt Marsh Nature Center.
Transport: B44 Bus to Avenue U/Nostrand Avenue

In an inlet between Gerritsen Beach and the Marine Park Golf Club, Mau Mau Island is an abandoned island about 0.7-miles-long that is completely man made. Like much of the south Brooklyn waterfront, the story of the island is rather trashy – that is, tied to garbage and landfill.

In 1917, Francis B. Pratt, son of the industrialist Charles Pratt (who founded Pratt Institute) and Alfred Tredway White, the Wall Street philanthropist behind Brooklyn Botanic Garden, donated 150 acres of land in south Brooklyn to be saved as natural marshland. White tragically died in 1921, but he would have been horrified to know what Robert Moses did on this land in the 1930s. With ocean dumping banned in New York City by the Supreme Court, Moses decided to take the city's trash to fill in marshlands. Using this method, he created Marine Park.

Mau Mau Island is just a nickname, albeit one that has stuck. It began life as White Island, another one of Robert Moses' trash landfills. In the book *The Other Islands of New York City*, Sharon Seitz and Stuart Miller write, "For years afterward, White Island's innards – banana peels, pieces of concrete, and newspapers referring to Dwight D. Eisenhower – leached into the creek." A temporary bridge was built to facilitate dumping of trash onto White Island. Robert Moses also layered sand on top of the garbage, a method that "unintentionally restored the coastal grassland habitat," writer Robert Sullivan says. The sand came from the excavation of the Belt Parkway, another Moses initiative. To prevent the sand from blowing onto the Marine Park Golf Club, opened in 1964, a layer of asphalt was added.

Neighbors called White Island a variety of nicknames – Golf Course Island, Gilligan's Island, and Mau Mau Island, after the Kenyan uprising of the 1950s. In 1974, New York City gave 1,024 acres of Marine Park to the National Parks Service to be included in the Gateway National Recreation Area, which included Mau Mau Island. An environmental restoration was supposed to have started in the late 1990s. Despite a decade of delay, work commenced in the 2000s, and in recent years, some of the grasslands and marshes have been restored to the island.

HARP AT FLOYD BENNETT FIELD

A hangar for aviation legends

50 Aviation Road, Brooklyn, NY 11234
www.nyharborparks.org
718-338-3799
Admission free
Tuesday, Thursday and Saturday 9am–4pm
Transport: 2 and 5 trains/Flatbush Av (be prepared for a very long walk, or bike the Greenway along Flatbush Avenue); bus: Q35 to the Park; car: Belt Parkway to Exit 11S, then Flatbush Avenue south to the main entrance

Floyd Bennett Field is the only area on a New York City map with nothing in it. On the ground it's a desert: wind rattles the fences, the hangars are abandoned relics with broken windows and the ghosts of military insignia fading on their faces. The airfield is vast stretches of concrete slab with orderly lines of weeds growing up through the cracks.

"No one knows about this place," says Bill, a former World War II pilot and volunteer at the Historical Aircraft Restoration Project (HARP). "It's a mystery."

HARP is headquartered in the field's Hangar B, which has become a free-form aviation museum. The walls are covered with clippings, photos, and paintings of great flying feats of the past, some of which took place right here: in its day, Floyd Bennett buzzed with legends. Opened in 1930 as New York's first municipal airport, the field couldn't compete with Newark, but its modern hangars attracted daredevils looking to break records. Roscoe Turner flew here, as did Charles Lindbergh and Amelia Earhart. Both Wiley Post and Howard Hughes started and ended fastest round-the-world flights on Floyd Bennett's runways.

Now Hangar B houses a score of restored aircraft, but the space is more than a museum: it's a sprawling workroom, with howling grinders and saws, and planes without wings, and wings without planes, and oiled engines sitting on metal stands. The principal smell is fresh paint.

"We're all volunteers," says Sol, a HARP member. "We come in three times a week and work on the planes, every group on a different aircraft." Sol gives a tour of the hangar; he has technical savvy born of affection, describing the machines as though they were people. The C-47 is reliable, a hard worker. The PBY Catalina won the war in the Pacific. Bill and his project partner Joseph wheel a freshly canvassed wing from a side room; they're restoring a Stearman biplane. ("You ever see the end of King Kong?" Joseph asks. "That one.") The men are old – Bill flew in Italy during the war, and Joseph was in training when it ended – and have lifetimes of aviation behind them. When they're finished with the Stearman, it will be given a fresh coat of bright yellow paint and added to the growing collection. "I would fly it," Joseph says, "except I don't trust the spars. You don't know what a spar is? C'mere, I'll show you ..."

DEAD HORSE BAY

What is durable in life: seashells, shoe soles, and glass

Southern side of the peninsula where Flatbush Avenue ends at the southeast corner of Brooklyn
Transport: Q35 bus from Brooklyn College, enter the Gateway National Recreation Area at the intersection of Aviation Road and Flatbush Avenue.

Just next to Floyd Bennett Field in Brooklyn sits Dead Horse Beach, whose macabre name aptly describes its history. Dead Horse Beach was once a separate island known as Barren Island, before the area was landfilled. But in recent years it has become more well-known as a hotspot for urban archaeology and scavenging. While officially the National Park Service does not condone the collecting of artifacts here, sifting through the beach is a walk back in time. The densely packed relics make the beach a landscape to behold and serves as a reminder of what humankind leaves behind, long after they themselves leave this earth.

Some finds date back to the early 1900s but more commonly you'll come across old Coca Cola bottles, medicine bottles and perfume bottles. Toy guns are not unusual, as are inadvertently gruesome discoveries like a decapitated doll head. Collectors have reportedly found old hand guns in the past. The rare plastic bottle that floats over forms an anachronistic, almost rude presence amongst the multi-colored bottles.

In 1859, the first horse rendering plants were constructed here which processed dead horses by boiling the bones down into glue. The remnants became commercial fertilizer. This was seen as a better alternative to the ongoing practice of leaving horse carcasses on New York City streets. Barren Island was considered ideal for this noxious activity because it was so remote, nobody would complain about the smell.

Later, the island was also used to deal with the city's garbage problem. Prior to the formation of the New York Sanitary Utilization Company, trash was dumped into the waterways. Motivated by financial reasons – the garbage was getting in the way of ship traffic – the city selected Barren Island for the processing and disposal of trash.

Similar to the horses, the trash would be boiled and steam-cooked until a layer of grease emerged at the top to be skimmed off and sold for industrial lubrication and soap. The stench, which could reach a radius of six to ten miles, would waft over to beach goers on Manhattan Beach where hotel evacuations would occur.

Unsurprisingly, neighboring communities began complaining and locals formed the Anti-Barren Island League. The landfill ceased operation in the 1940s and was capped off in 1953, but the waste emerges on a daily basis due to erosion, leaving a beach of strewn bottles, old toys, and shoes.

ALPHABETICAL INDEX

ALPHABETICAL INDEX

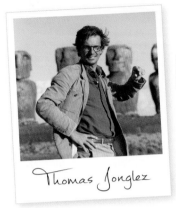

Thomas Jonglez

t was September 1995 and Thomas Jonglez was in Peshawar, the northern Pakistani city 20 kilometres from the tribal zone he was to visit a few days later. It occurred to him that he should record the hidden aspects of his native city, Paris, which he knew so well. During his seven-month trip back home from Beijing, the countries he crossed took him in Tibet (entering clandestinely, hidden under blankets in an overnight bus), Iran and Kurdistan. He never took a plane but travelled by boat, train or bus, hitchhiking, cycling, on horseback or on foot, reaching Paris just in time to celebrate Christmas with the family.

On his return, he spent two fantastic years wandering the streets of the capital to gather material for his first "secret guide", written with a friend. For the next seven years he worked in the steel industry until the passion for discovery overtook him. He launched Jonglez Publishing in 2003 and moved to Venice three years later.

In 2013, in search of new adventures, the family left Venice to spend six months in Brazil, via North Korea, Micronesia, the Solomon Islands, Easter Island, Peru and Bolivia.

He now lives in Rio de Janeiro with his wife and three children. Jonglez Publishing produces a range of titles in nine languages, released in 30 countries.

ACKNOWLEDGEMENTS:

Michelle and Augustin would like to thank the following people for their assistance with this book: Justin Rivers, Laurie Gwen Shapiro, Jeff Reuben, Diana Huang, Hannah Frishberg, Alyssa Loorya of Chrysalis Archaeological Consultants, John Cortese and family, Luke Spencer, Corey William Schneider, Miriam Kelly, Dennis Vouderis of Deno's Wonder Wheel, the New York Transit Museum, Rabbi Shaul Shimon Deutsch of Torah Animal World and the Living Torah Museum, Tom Miskel of the Park Slope Veterans Museum, the Park Slope Armory YMCA, the Port Authority of New York and New Jersey and Tania Duvergne with the NYC School Construction Authority. In addition, we would like to thank the entire team of our company, Untapped Cities, for their inspiration and support, and all the friends and family who came exploring with us every weekend in Brooklyn.

This book is dedicated to Charlotte, our explorer, who was born in Brooklyn.

PHOTOGRAPHY CREDITS:

Pictures by Augustin Pasquet. Additional photos by Michelle Young. Photographs of Bergen Street subway station by @Vic.Invades on Instagram, Magnolia Grandiflora photograph by Jim Henderson, Photos of Erasmus Hall as noted. Photographs by T.M. Rives for entries listed below.

ADDITIONAL WRITING CREDIT:

The following entries were written by T.M. Rives and were originally published in *Secret New York* and *Secret New York: Curious Activities*. Some entries have been edited or updated.

Prison Ship Martyrs Monument, "Lost Columbus" of Cadman Plaza, Masstransiscope, Metropolitan Championship, Seining in the East River, Fliers' And Explorers' Globe, 58 Joralemon Street, The Doors of Our Lady of Lebanon, Plymouth Rock at Plymouth Church, The City Reliquary, Brooklyn Grange, 770 Eastern Parkway, Sukkhot, Fragrance Garden at Brooklyn Botanic, Canoeing the Gowanus Canal, Warren Place, Faith Mosque, Quaker Cemetery, Eruvin, The New Utrecht Liberty Pole, Topsy Memorial, Polar Bear Plunge, Kayak in Jamaica Bay, Harp at Floyd Bennett Field

Maps: Cyrille Suss - **Layout design:** Coralie Cintrat - **Layout:** Alessio Melandri and Stéphanie Benoit - **Editing:** Matt Gay - **Proofreading:** Eleni Salemi - **Publishing:** Clémence Mathé

© JONGLEZ 2019
Registration of copyright: February 2019 – Edition: 02
ISBN: 978-2-36195-312-6
Printed in Bulgaria by Dedrax